RETURNING TO THE CAMINO FRANCES

French Way of the Camino de Santiago

Richard Davis

CONTENTS

Title Page	
Authors Note	1
Dedication	2
Returning to the Camino Frances	3
London to St Jean Pied De Port	12
St Jean Pied de Port to Roncesvalles	16
Roncesvalles to Zubiri	19
Zubiri to Pamplona	22
Pamplona to Puento Laren	24
Puente Laren to Estella	27
Estella to Los Argos.	29
Burgos Rest Day	31
Burgos rest day	35
Burgos to San Bol	37
San Bol to Boadilla del Camino	40
Boadilla del Camino to Carrión de los Conde	44
Carrión de Los Conde to Moratinos	46
Moritanos to Bercianos del Real	50
Bercianos del Real to Leon	54
Leon to Villar de Mazarife	58
Villar de Mazarife to Astorga	61

Astorga to Rabanal del Camino	65
Rabanal del Camino to Molinaseca	67
Molinaseca to Villafranca	71
Villafranca to La Faba	75
La Faba to Triacastela	78
Triacastela to Sarria	80
Sarria to Portomarin	83
Portomarin to Palais del Rei	86
Palais del Rei to Azura	89
Azura to Lavacolla	93
Lavacolla to Santiago de Compostela	97
My Reflections	103

AUTHORS NOTE

This account shouldn't be taken as a blueprint or advice for anyone considering walking the many routes of the Camino Santiago de Compostela. Each experience is very unique and individual and there are many determining factors that include the level of accommodation chosen which may depend upon your budget and the desired distance walked each day or indeed the speed of pace. There are many decisions made by each pilgrim that determine the overall outcome but the greatest reward I believe comes from the varied characters that you'll encounter each day.

John Brierley is mentioned throughout this work because of his expertise of all things Camino related. I received a kind email from John prior to my walking where he said he would read this account if time allowed, sadly John died whilst I was writing up these notes but I hope he would have approved of my honest ramblings.

For amusement purposes I've included my daily walking steps and a brief mention of my evening meals. I hope you find the following thought provoking and at times comical.

DEDICATION

JOYCE DAVIS

14th September 1933 to 6th April 2022

My Mum who taught me by example never to doubt God's presence.

RETURNING TO THE CAMINO FRANCES

(French Way of the Camino de Santiago)

Forward

In 2014 I had a life changing experience. I didn't "find God", I've always known and felt his presence despite not being devout, perhaps I should be! He has always been there when I'm most in need and has shown himself through my mother in particular and other loved ones. I didn't alter my domestic arrangements with a new life partner or a new career path or a house move, nor did I recover from a serious illness and so on the face of it it's hard to make my "life changing" statement or for others to appreciate it. What I did in the Spring of 2014 was to set off on a walking pilgrimage route, the "Camino de Santiago". There are several routes for the "Way of St James" but I chose the most established and popular one that is the French route of 500 miles which begins in the small town of St. Jean Pied de Port in the Basque area of the Pyrenees and then traverses across northern Spain through the cities of Pamplona, Logrono, Burgos, Leon and culminates at Santiago de Compostela where the bones of St James, the disciple of Christ, can be found.

Like many of my fellow pilgrims and walkers I was in need of some sense of spiritual awareness, a need to reflect on my life and find peace and understanding away from the problems of modern life. I suspect this is what many would refer to as "time out" or recharging the batteries or many other overused clichés. My father had been diagnosed with Alzheimer's causing distress to his loved ones who in turn endlessly repeated the same answer to his one and only question, "where's mum?" Fortunately with a loving and supportive wife and a close family they all agreed that the Camino pilgrimage was a terrific idea and as the departure date loomed nearer my brother Chris decided to join me by walking from the Pilgrim office in St Jean Pied de Port to Legrono, the first seven day leg of a thirty three day hike depending on one's walking pace. His circumstances did change in 2014, perhaps he would say dramatically in a life changing manner, when he resigned from a busy professional career as an accountant deciding to opt for a life of semi-retirement and of more relaxing enjoyment. Like me he had family support and so with great excitement and nervous anticipation we set off over the channel passing through Paris and heading by train south to the Pyrenees.

On arrival in Paris when boarding the underground train I knew that in the weeks to come I would be out of my "comfort zone", forced to share accommodation and washing areas, communal kitchens and dining rooms. I would need ear plugs to sleep whilst others, literally within spitting distance, snored, grunted and made embarrassing noises only to be laughed at now in politically incorrect and dated 'British Carry On' films. I was, and still am, a reserved Englishman but I'd read the guide books warning me of the shared living conditions and like most other walkers I had watched the film, "The Way", the Martin Sheen movie responsible for the growing popularity of the French Camino Pilgrimage. I knew that I would need to become more sociable and most importantly tolerant in the days ahead in order to survive the ordeal of living amongst strangers in such close proximity and therefore when I saw a travelling pilgrim proudly displaying a Scallop shell, the sign of a fellow pilgrim of St James, on the Paris Metro I bravely struck up a conversation. A German civil servant and housewife smiled back immediately, noticing my own shell picked up from a local beach near me in Rye Sussex. Birgit from Essen in Germany spoke very good English especially when compared to my pigeon German that was only of use if ordering a beer, coffee or ice cream. She had one of the kindest natures

I have ever encountered and accompanied me the entire length of the Camino journey and we entered the Basilica in Santiago de Compostela together. My brother on the train, as we headed for Bayonne, had the same experience befriending an Australian nun named Leone from the Ursuline order living in Sydney Australia. She was also clearly a pilgrim with a backpack laden down with clothing and washing supplies, it would be unusual for any backpacker on this train heading south not to be a pilgrim destined for the pilgrim Camino route. Further confirmation if needed was the scallop shell of St James, in memory of the Spanish patron Saint whose remains were miraculously brought from the sea by crustaceans and now resting in a silver casket in Galicia, hung proudly from her backpack. We became a group of four instantly good companions on the Camino and remain friends to this day with our shared memories and experiences from this magical moment in time, four or five weeks, in my case, away from life's mix of mundane domesticity and stress.

There was a familiar routine to each day's trek. Regardless of what time you'd set your travel clock or wristwatch alarm in the Albergue or hostel you would be woken early by creaking beds, loud intakes of breath, coughing and yawning and this cacophony was soon followed by the arrival of a lone torch light. Then the rustling of sleeping bags being rolled up as tightly as possible to be forced into an already bulging rucksack. It was time to stir oneself and do likewise as in the certain knowledge that the ceiling lights would soon be on to prevent accidents or mishaps from those alighting from their top bunk beds and needing to find safe footing on the ladder rungs. Whether further sleep was required or not would be immaterial! The morning cold air would soon hit your face as the first strides of the day began and most conversations would be brief, simply centering around how successful each other's nights sleep had been amongst the now familiar snoring and involuntary excesses of bodily air.

After an hour or perhaps two, assuming you were fortunate

with dry weather that might delay your departure, you would experience the warmth of the rising sun and then with fellow pilgrims now more talkative you would arrive at a breakfast destination. Rucksacks, walking poles and possibly boots would be left outside the selection of small cafés strategically situated along 'The Way' and a much needed strong Spanish coffee with pastries, tortillas and fresh orange juice would rejuvenate the waking body and limbs for the second stage of the day's labours. With periodic breaks thereafter one would walk for a further five hours or so before arriving at a chosen town or village where you might have decided it to be your night's resting place. One would check in, have your credential passport stamped, make your pilgrim payment or donation, take a shower (often cold) and wash your sweaty and dusty clothes from the day in often cracked or stained sinks in the communal garden areas. Many pilgrims would then briefly sleep, others would make repairs to their blistering feet while the seasoned pilgrim might make a visit to the local church or Basilica before the inevitable meeting up place of bars, cafes and restaurants for the 'Pellegrino dish of the day'. The evening meal often started with a bowl of soup and bread, and as I recall ended with a 'cream caramel' that the Spanish bizarrely refer to on English written menus as a "flan". It was during these moments of forced communal living that wider friendships were formed in what was at the beginning of my Camino a daunting prospect, of living like children away from their parents with their first camping school trip. Indeed having been spared the "English Public School" experience I can imagine that the Camino pilgrim life in its infancy is akin to the nervousness and fear felt of a child being sent away to imposing and fearful Gothic buildings with large dormitories, certainly the often reputed 'cold showers' and school dinners of many childhood memories I suspect are true of the Way of St James!

With each passing day the four of us grew closer and the communal living that had been so worrying for my shy nature became possibly the most enjoyable and informative part of the

Camino experience. We each relied on the other's talents as our German friend spoke some Spanish, my brother's navigation skills were useful with his excellent "John Brierly" guide in hand and the sense of heavenly goodness combined at times with a mischievous humour was a constant in the Australian nun. I recall a conversation where I said how fortunate I was to be walking with such a kind group whilst I contributed nothing, she simply and kindly stated.
"God wants us to live in communities Richard, not alone!" It was enough to reassure me of my presence being as welcomed by her as any other and her delivery so soft and yet direct that I felt instantly at ease. There were others who became close fellow pilgrims on the periphery of our tight group, three friendly Australians from Brisbane that I am still in touch with mostly when England met Australia on the cricket field and recently a trip to Sweden where one of the three now lives with his newly married wife, also a veteran pilgrim. A retiree from Canada, another German girl, a jocular Englishman living in America and a Dutch man from a strange province who proudly boasted that his kinsman of the Netherlands don't mix well. His lone presence was the one exception to the friendly Camino and a reminder that this wasn't quite Utopia or the Garden of Eden!

During the long days of walking the conversations became more free flowing, relaxed and after a short while the content was more personal in nature. If you walk, eat and share bedrooms in such close and confined conditions it becomes inevitable that you will get to know each other well, perhaps this is the hidden magic of the Camino that in the forced presence of others the boundaries of social niceties and politeness are broken down very quickly. In a very short while one finds oneself at ease and indeed when an unknown pilgrim arrives with a faster pace from behind or of a slowing down from one ahead conversations are entered into quickly once you have learnt their name and the country where they are domiciled. Discussions from this point on are rarely strained or awkward. The Camino is the best of all 'social levellers' and yet it must be said the daily walking is also attractive for those seeking peace and solitude, a knowing smile is sufficient to alert other pilgrims of a wish to walk with one's own thoughts and for pleasantries to be shared later often over the evening meal.

Whilst walking across the hot Messeta two weeks into my 2014 trek I was bitten by a large buzzing hornet that entered my Polo shirt via the open neck and once on my back was out of my reach to allow it an easy escape. In the hornet's attempt to free himself from the tight cavity squeezed by my rucksack straps I had been bitten twice, that afternoon without my requesting nursing assistance the kind German friend saw the angry bites on my return from the communal showers and applied some ointment to the red swollen and angry bite marks. At the point of my embarking on the Camino, if someone had said that in two weeks time I would find a stranger rubbing soothing ointment onto my back then my English reserved nature would not have believed it possible. It was events such as this and the many others that would make the Camino so memorable and that would stay with me, I believe for a lifetime, and that I would state is a "life changing" experience and one that I would recommend to all others.

The Camino can be addictive. To walk each day without a care in the world other than the only consideration being of where I will find myself by mid-afternoon and sleeping that night after the day's long trek is a liberating sensation. Will the accommodation be comfortable and clean, will the evening meal be pleasant, will there be great humour as there had been each night since arriving at the start and who might join or leave the fringes of our group whether it be pre planned or through a lack of stamina or perhaps injury. Once one had walked for three or four days and with good fortune be free of blisters or other walking repetitive injuries you would soon know whether your feet and body would be able to withstand the next thirty days and so this initial worry would leave a state of spiritual contentment and escapism.

There is always the possibility of a twisted ankle or a fall from a badly balanced and ill fitting rucksack but these thoughts are far from your mind once you are successfully underway and you are mentally determined to receive your Compostela, the certificate of achievement for some, or Heavenly forgiveness for others upon completion at the Santiago de Compostela pilgrim office.

Is this "escapism" healthy or is it a "fool's paradise"? Is it fair on my supportive wife for me to vanish for a month of what many would call another holiday? Of course I have her permission and the trust that my behaviour would be of a good pilgrim! I haven't read 'Chaucer's Canterbury Tales' where I understand the stories told by pilgrims are perhaps a bit more lively than the late night chatting that I encountered. It's very unlikely that I would act like a drunkard on a youthful holiday in the sunny Mediterranean and yet still being a man with the same human failings as any other I can obviously be tempted! The Camino I believe answers this issue, to walk daily for up to thirty kilometres by nightfall one can only sleep in often crowded dormitories, the sleep of an innocent, until the lone torch and morning rustling alerts you to walk once more. Attachments are formed, as I said how could they not be but they are, in my experience, attachments around a mutual understanding of what the pilgrimage is, a powerful sense of spiritual uplifting and with this shared acceptance you do nothing other than walk on with God's grace and encouraged by fellow pilgrims finding yourself on occasion discussing your deepest innermost thoughts. Perhaps one should look at the issue of attachments the other way around, the wrong attachments are those that we physically or mentally make prior to a pilgrimage and that one perhaps laments and asks for contrition by walking the Camino where we hope to be forgiven and healed from self inflicted heartache.

In the knowledge that you walk the Camino not for heightened earthly pleasures or excesses of vice, despite the fine and less costly wine, one still has to consider why I am now planning another Camino pilgrimage? Surely once was enough my sensible inner voice tells me! I have my Compostela, the document of achievement and forgiveness of a mortal sin which is the opinion of some devout Catholics and who am I to say this isn't the case. Perhaps I need more than one indulgence or forgiveness! The truth is that when I arrived at Santiago de Compostela and on the way I found inner peace. The swinging incense burner, amongst the mass of pilgrims, swaying from either side of the Naive above the amazed congregation sending smokey fumes into the air whilst the heavenly sound of a singing nun filling the Basilica is how I imagine the very peace of Heaven to be. Pilgrims gather to witness the presence of God, each in select groups amongst their new found friends, brothers and sisters with a sense that they are truly blessed and rewarded for their tiring efforts in walking the many pilgrimage routes to this spot. The experience is the crowning glory of the Camino and as I said, it's addictive!

As I write this forward in the depths of Winter of 2022 I am beginning my preparations for "Returning to the Camino Frances", I must make sure my boots are as comfortable as the ones used before, that during the nine years since my last long period of daily walking I haven't lost the level of fitness required and I must make the necessary travel arrangements. I must, when the time comes, have courage that once more I will be forced to meet strangers and tell myself that there is decency in the human condition and that I will once again find kindness. I will kiss my wife Kathy and reassure her of my safe return and have trust and faith that she will be well during my absence. I'll tell myself that the Camino is a calling from God to replenish my body, soul and faith in the goodness of people and humanity which is so evidently sadly lacking with each news bulletin that fills every moment of our current lives. Regardless of faith or motive I believe all should be encouraged to walk the Camino routes for uplifting reflection, to spend time in the company of others also looking for a heightened experience and in doing so find the better side of their own nature. What follows are my daily reflections and account of "Returning to the Camino Frances"

Giant statue of a Pilgrim, Pedrafita do Cebreiro

LONDON TO ST JEAN PIED DE PORT

7628 Steps

Cod Stew And French Fries. Vin Rouge.

As I wake from my London hotel, opposite Kings Cross station, any lingering doubts I may have as to walking the Camino once more are dispelled having switched on the breakfast television news. The mainstream media outlets endlessly and enthusiastically report the escalating war in Ukraine, that Pope Francis called "senseless", without any discussion of peace talks or a solution that is obviously needed to avoid the unthinkable! Therefore, a month away from the frenzy of depressing news media outlets will do me no harm. The Eurostar train will take me in comfort through the tunnel to Paris and after a short underground metro trip to Montparnasse station I will then journey south to Bayonne and the town of St Jean Pied De Port. With the same nervous anticipation mixed with excitement that I felt nine years ago I switch off the offending television and make my way to the Eurostar platform of Saint Pancras station below the Champagne bar which at this early hour is sensibly shut. My pilgrim lifestyle has begun, fizzy bubbles will return when I'm back on English soil I tell myself!

Standing on the crowded Metro underground it occurs to me that directly above my head is a fierce reenactment of the French Revolution from 1789, the peasants are once more rioting hurling cobblestones as their forebears had done before but this time they include more modern projectiles. Refuse bins, E scooters, and anything that can be set alight or lifted from the ground is being thrown towards the Gendarmerie who reply with tear gas, water canon and baton charges, thankfully not the live ammunition and cavalry charges with drawn swords of previous times prior to the successful storming of the Bastille. Clearly this is not the start to the Camino I'd hoped for or akin to the one so enjoyable nine years before so what is causing the anger from the Parisians on the streets above? Surely we've become a better society since the uprising of two hundred and fifty years ago, surely the unrest isn't a desperate plea for bread from those at their wits end with empty bellies and bare feet wearing rags and living in squalor! No, they aren't hungry, they aren't desperate for healthcare although perhaps having to wait in turn, they aren't witnessing their children dying through malnutrition or suffering in pain from disease or illnesses now a footnote of misery and human suffering consigned to the history books. Their gripe, their fury, their rage and protest is the prospect of an extra two years employment before a benevolent state pension can be taken to live out their lives in relative comfort. A strong contrast when compared to the Parisians who lived through revolution and the "terror" whilst watching the guillotine violently drop delivering justice and retribution. But who am I to judge these angry modern day protesters as I hope my troublesome and disruptive train strike threatened journey through Paris will soon be a distant memory. I'm sure the magic of my Camino walk will mellow my mood and I'll develop an understanding tolerance towards these angry peasants and their cause! I'll certainly reflect once more on my emotions and feelings of this experience whilst travelling through Paris at the end of this book so please read on!

Finally I boarded the Bayonne train and with relief settled back in my reserved seat on the last train out of Paris before a day of national strikes was due to start. A large late middle aged French lady came swaying up the aisle laden down with bags on either side in my direction and pretended that she spoke no English after taking a fancy to my window seat. My French was too poor to argue so I used a universal sign pointing clearly to the number displayed above my seat with corresponding evidence on the ticket in my hand. Sadly it was obvious she wouldn't back down despite the screamingly clear evidence I had shown her. I should have said, "sacre bleu, madam. Je suis asseoir ici!" But no, I acquiesced and she immediately became grateful in my mother tongue of English. Fortunately the journey went well from here and it was a relief to be underway and then followed by a successful change of train at Bayonne and I was soon enjoying the scenery around St Jean Pied de Port very reminiscent of Snowdonia in Wales or the Scottish Highlands. After my difficult experience in Paris and on the train I'm beginning to understand the cause of Basque separatism. I mischievously tell myself having been seduced by the contrast of the beautiful countryside against the angry city.

Arriving at my Gite accommodation I met a young Dublin chap named Donnacha who was allocated the bunk bed above me and later I was introduced to his brother Cormac staying in a different hostel but also with the intention of walking the following day. We found a restaurant and within the space of a half hour the Camino delivered its magic once more, two more familiar faces from the Bayonne to St Jean Pied de Port train journey arrived and then a third, a Taiwanese lady named Tongi now living in Vienna with an interesting tale to tell. Donnacha was between employment positions and with spare time on his hands before marriage, perhaps encouraged by his fiancé who had previously undertaken the walk, was good company. Tongi was a costume designer for the film industry and clearly cultured with a knowledge of the arts, music and literature. Instinctively I can tell her character is gentle as she tells me about the Budist faith she would adopt if compelled, she clearly had a kindness of heart. Cormac was obviously in a holiday mood and I suspect completely unprepared for what was to come from the Camino experience. I was wrong subsequently to believe he would find the difficulties of the walk so overwhelming that his attempt would end prematurely, his white training shoes became muddied and dirty, his blisters large and angry, his backpack obviously inadequate and yet he stayed on the Camino route but what brought the greatest surprise was his earthy humour and laughter in adversity fuelled by the excesses of beer, wine and youthfulness. I couldn't help but admire and warm to his character.

Returning to the Gite I knew that the following morning I would depart early in good company and it occurred to me that this group could indeed walk with me until the very end and in doing so remain lifelong friends. And yet it was obviously too early to tell as each of us whilst fighting fit on the eve of tomorrow's long walk to the monastery of Roncesvalles couldn't foresee what difficulties would come. A much needed eight hours of sleep will render the passing through Paris a distant memory and tomorrow will bring the first physical challenge, a six hour hike that will be the first test and indication of the extent of my ageing decline and my ability to walk the entire Camino distance from this starting point.

ST JEAN PIED DE PORT TO RONCESVALLES

34431 steps

Chicken And Chips Vin Rouge

Day one turned out to be an extremely difficult walk with a steep incline over the last 10 Kilometres, the Napoleon route over the top is much more dangerous in altitude with a risk of snow until April 1st and so we poor innocent Pilgrims are forbidden from the higher routes and forced to take the way with less danger but a more strenuous and as it turned out annoying final stretch. This was particularly difficult to accept in the knowledge that there was no snow over the Pyranese in this warmest of winters just passed, the wintry conditions of this Camino were on their way! It was here on the final slope that I first encountered a mother and daughter, Jo and Katie from Yorkshire England, and Katie's overwhelming kindness. She gave me some of her drinking water along with sugar sweets for energy as the incline at the end of the day was taking its toll on all around. What made Katie's kindness to me so surprising was that she was attending to her mother who was beginning to suffer hip pain from the steep incline and was therefore relaying both her rucksack and her mother's up the seemingly never ending slope. How much easier would it have been to walk the Napoleon route in the baking hot conditions where the gradient was kinder and ample water fountains are found with well placed resting areas already well established supplying needed goodies for the day's walk in relative comfort. Katie's benevolence was yet more evidence of the Camino kind spirit that was so familiar from my previous experience.

The toil and arduous walk sadly detracted from the beauty of the scenery and it was a relief to arrive at Roncesvalles for two hours of relaxation before the evening Pelegrino meal of the predictable and in my case anticipated Chicken and Chips. The step count today doesn't do justice to the sheer pain barrier that we all walked through, every Camino day from now on will be easier I tell myself! Two pilgrims have joined our group and to my amazement I question what are the odds, not only are they Englishmen but they are fine Kentish lads named Charles and Nick from Sittingbourne and Gravesend respectively living in areas I know well from my home county and along with the Dublin brothers and Tangi we all slept well in the huge monastery building. The Kentish lads and I share many connections and despite there being some twenty years difference in age and attitudes it's enjoyable to discuss the pubs and clubs that we all frequented albeit with many years between the libations and a generation apart.

Monastero di Roncisvalle

RONCESVALLES TO ZUBIRI

35428 Steps

Cod And Chips Vino Tinto

Rising early and underway I have twinges of discomfort in the toe area of my right boot and aches in my calves from the unexpected difficult climb of the day before. I tell myself all will be well from the training I'd undertaken prior to the start and therefore I grit my teeth and put my best foot forward. I walked for the second day running with Donnacha and his surprisingly quiet brother today, Cormac, who at times lagged behind, perhaps the cause being the early morning departure or more likely the extra bottle of wine he'd consumed at dinner the night before. The Dublin brothers' accents are very strong, broad and delivered at great speed and after a while I felt awkward in persistently asking them to repeat themselves but on reflection it occurred to me that they too may be experiencing the same problem with my south east English local dialogue.

Over the first two hours of the day and whilst completely distracted discussing Arsenal's prospects of winning the Premier League we took a wrong turn at Valcarlos, the first small town that one encounters after the Roncesvalles monastery, which was particularly annoying for me having walked the same route nine years prior. I was concerned that my physical ability may not be adequate for the challenge of the Camino but at no point did I believe my mental capacity could be an issue! Could I mischievously blame the Dublin boys for my lack of attention, could I humorously make the connection between the Irish brothers being to blame as part of the stereotypical characters of simple Leprechauns! No, of course not. These Irish brothers who at times made no sense to my confused ears and slow understanding are intelligent lads with professional careers in engineering and accountancy and the mistake of walking so far of course is mine and mine alone. However the resulting attempt to rectify the error was shared, the Irish lads did what all youngsters do when searching for an answer and eagerly turned to their mobile phone APPS. A further delay and mistake followed as the boys swore blind that an earlier missed right turning would lead us back to the way; it didn't and became obvious as we walked over a cattle grid and were met with a barbed wire fence! I smiled later once the mistakes were rectified and we were back on the well marked path but in the moment and in realisation of an extra five miles added to the day it wasn't much fun. My mood improved and we met up with two Japanese sisters cheerfully walking along in the summer sunshine but my feet weren't so contented, a throbbing from the toes alerted me to the worry that problems could be looming ahead! Twenty Three Kilometres turned out to be nearer Thirty but despite being tired and the foot discomfort I feel on completion of this second day fit in my body and hoping that a good soaking and a well placed plaster would heal the developing blisters and solve the problem.

In the Zubiri Albergue I met a pleasant Canadian chap called Lochlan from Toronto, a Swiss German chap called Mark and a French girl from Lille named Valentine who looks remarkably familiar to a famous French film actress. We enjoyed a good evening meal but I decided against too much Vino Tinto as the many years since my last Camino have taken their toll making the socialising aspect of evening excesses unwise. Beer, wine and my newly diagnosed gluten intolerance definitely make the overindulgence of the past a daunting possibility if repeated and I therefore believe for obvious reasons that this Camino experience may be very different.

I met more amiable pilgrims post dinner, how amazing to find myself in a Spanish bar with a French girl Valentine from Lille, a multilingual Danish man named Jack from Copenhagen, Sophie from the Netherlands, Lochlan from Toronto Canada, Mikel from Jutland Denmark, Paula a youngster from Madrid Spain who spoke a little Basque if required, two friendly South Korean girls, a Belgium girl Maria recently qualified in something that didn't easily translate into English, two Italian youngsters and me. Were they being kind, speaking about their Camino plans and adventures in English, my language, were they genuinely interested in my tales of the pilgrimage nearly ten years before? Most likely the youngsters spoke English because it was to each of them their shared second common language taught in their schools and they would have all watched British and American television shows. However I'm in such a relaxed mood to fool myself that for the benefit of Lachlan and I and fueled with Camino good spirit that it was our sparkling personalities that brought the group to communal harmony and enjoyment!

ZUBIRI TO PAMPLONA

27331 steps

Tapas And A Mixed Selection Of Liberal Camino Hospitality

The day started with a lovely walk out of Zubiri once I had passed the cement works on the right hand side. The walk meanders along the valley and the weather was very pleasant for the stroll that was mostly on flat terrain. I was in a good mood and every now and again encountered new and recognisable pilgrims from the previous two days but sadly my mood was about to change, not because of the forecasted rain that didn't materialise but from another unexpected and I would argue horrifying sight. A rough area and encampment of squalor on the outskirts of Pamplona was to be the lowest point of my Camino and a lasting memory that left me disgusted by my fellow man. Amongst the filth and dregs a man of middle age and wearing a filthy light brown vest and dirty jogging bottoms was kicking a horse whilst holding its reins from the front. At least three high kicks beat against the grey animal either side of its fleshy area above its front legs. If I were in England I would certainly have phoned the police or even investigated myself with telephone mobile video footage for evidence to alert the RSPCA but I have to accept that perhaps the Mediterranean psyche isn't as friendly towards animals. Indeed the Spanish culture takes delight in brutality towards bulls and allows dogs to be chained up hour on end in the hot sun so what hope would I have of this despicable man being punished for his crime if he were reported. Added to which the squalor of the encampment suggested it was a community of "travellers" and rather like many other countries I suspect, perhaps wrongly, believe this community has a completely different set of rules that the establishment and usual norms of behaviour turn a blind eye to! In this singular moment my troubled conscience would have loved to have witnessed the horse kick the man in his groyne or preferably head and cause mortal pain. Will my Camino experience on completion give me a greater degree of tolerance towards this man? Please read on to see!

The group from the previous day have all made it to the same Albergue next to the Cathedral and so a good evening will surely follow once I've looked around the town and tried to erase the memory of the animal cruelty that I'd witnessed which sadly remains and inevitably affected my mood. However the dinner was one full of cheer and the evening could have resulted in a monster drinking session and lead to a monumental hangover the following morning that would have ruined the walk for the next two days. Vino Tinto, beer and other delights were offered by the multinational Peligrinos and I resisted as best I could which thankfully should be enough to get enjoyment from tomorrow's walk which is a planned Twenty Three Kilometres. I really like this varied group of wonderful pilgrims, they are idealistic and charitable people each with a career path set out of benevolence and decency. Their youthfulness is infectious, kind and their acceptance of my presence amongst them despite my more cynical and hardened character scarred by the disappointments of life is reassuring. This group isn't yet angry, as I and some of my generation have become with humanity that has arguably failed us to create disunity and division at home or abroad. These youngsters don't have the cautious approach to life that comes with age and I'm left wondering how they would have reacted had they witnessed the attack upon the horse that I had. I had no intention of broaching the subject with them to find out and in doing so perhaps ruin the Camino mood of this enjoyable evening!

PAMPLONA TO PUENTO LAREN

35539 Steps

Pork Loin and Chips

The first half of the day is uphill and the second stage a steep decline after the plateau where we pass the windmills at the top looking back at the beautiful views towards Pamplona. I slept well despite the creaking metal bed frame that partially woke me each time I moved or the tossing and turning of the late arrival of an unknown pilgrim above me. Fortunately the charming South Korean sisters opposite me later said they had slept well with no noticeable sound of snoring from any of us in the vicinity. We woke early as is the Camino way and were soon underway with the morning sunrise seeing us remove clothing layers, it was a pleasant stroll out of Pamplona and then followed by the difficult walk up to the top of Alto del Perdon. At the top and away from any shelter we encountered the cold strong breeze once more preventing any lengthy period of rest. I would have stayed longer enjoying the views but after the customary photos I left for the downward stage chatting with Eddie from Australia and Donnacha mostly about cricket, Dublin life and the Camino in general. Eddie was a seasoned Camino veteran, he had been diagnosed with a heart condition and advised to lose weight from his doctor and so supplied with medication was now embarking on his eighth Camino.

The descent was steep in places but comfortable and so I was surprised to see a new blister forming on another toe of my right foot, I suspect caused by the brutal climb up to Roncesvalles that I discussed in the earlier stage. This could stop the Camino in its tracks if it becomes worse but I'm hoping the cold waters of a running stream at the Puente Laren Albergue will deliver a miracle cure! I've managed so far to keep up with the friendly youngsters on the Way mostly by having interesting conversations that enable one to walk through any pain and on this particular leg of the Camino stroll I talked to Bethany, a trainee Psychiatrist from Washington DC. She chatted with an air of optimism and hope and spoke of the need for many to have counselling for the trauma faced in society whether it be from army veterans suffering from PTSD or children from troubled backgrounds. In particular she discussed the need to avoid being judgmental which is a central part of the psychiatry profession. I could tell she would be highly regarded and successful in her chosen field. I later chatted to Jack, for the final part of the day's walk until the arrival, a social worker from Copenhagen who I mentioned above and once more I was heartened by his enthusiasm and approach to his career choice of helping vulnerable young adults with special needs. Jack has amazing social skills, possibly as a result of his profession, he has the ability to put one and all at ease and therefore the time passed quickly and before long we arrived in the beautiful town of Puento Laren. The twelve assembled pilgrims all enjoyed another evening of friendly conversation over a communal dinner with outside seating of a restaurant against the backdrop of the flowing river passing by before retiring for the night's sleep. On this occasion I'm in an upper bunk bed above Jack and despite the heat and noise of the overcrowded dormitory I slept well.

Magical views leaving Estella

PUENTE LAREN TO ESTELLA

33861 Steps

Lomo Bacon, Chips And Green Pepper

It was a really good and enjoyable initial part of the day with an uphill walk as I tried not to dwell on the ever present throbbing and tightness felt in my right foot whilst I chatted with Daniel, a software engineer from Barcelona. Our conversations were very varied from the Sophists of Ancient Greece to weight loss whilst walking the Camino and his hopes to ultimately be a successful chef which perhaps explained the excess weight issues that we both have. He is younger than me but we have a great deal in common, not least a love of good food and a questioning attitude towards accepting the propaganda of mainstream media. He was adamant that there were two sides and arguments to the rights and wrongs of the Spanish civil war when I suggested that our history books and culture generally only teaches the wonderful exploits of Hemmingway and the International Brigade. Daniel also explained as best he could the issue of Catalan separatism and the recent referendum on independence that saw the Spanish government and authorities clamp down on the movement's leaders. Slightly related to this was our United Kingdom decision to leave the European Union where I agreed with Daniel there were varying arguments and not the offensive terminology that brands leavers as "populist"!

The ground levelled off and the walk passed over minor dips and inclines until a brief rain shower appeared, a Basque cycle race passed along the road above us and we soon found ourselves nearing Estella where we were joined once more by Jack, Tongi and Valentine.

We all spent the afternoon relaxing in conversation whilst washing clothes followed by a stroll around the town where the cycle race once more appeared accompanied by cheering crowds and well wishers. I later was informed that the race was a big Basque event and named after a famous cyclist who apparently was watching on and awarding the prize. The evening meal was yet more fun where fourteen of us gathered and despite two Spaniards at our table the waiter was confused by the simplest of orders. How wonderful that fourteen pilgrims from nine nationalities can sit enjoying the ambience and Camino spirit. The joke of the elderly Dane opposite me about sleeping the previous evening with a mother and daughter from England, Jo and Katie brought great laughter. Perhaps this is the nearest we came to one of Chaucer's Tales! We all knew that he meant in the same room with twin bunk beds but couldn't resist allowing his puzzling translation to run its course encouraged by Cormac!

ESTELLA TO LOS ARGOS.

30687 Steps

Gluten Free Pizza and Chips

The forecasted rain didn't materialise and it was a beautiful walk through green fields whilst watching the gentle breezes sway through the wheat and barley fields with the sun periodically breaking through the moving clouds. A rainbow touched the mountains in the distance holding my attention whilst an Englishman named Nigel tried to entertain me with lengthy anecdotes of his attempts to teach science to disruptive secondary pupils back home. After a lengthy café visit where I nursed my blistering toes and spent a prolonged period over my cafe con leche Nigel accepted the fact that he didn't have a captive audience and so left me to finish my now stone cold drink.

The final and most enjoyable part of the day was meeting once more the retired NHS radiographer named Jo and her daughter Katie who I'd met on the first eventful day but on that occasion the toil required for the walk prevented any discussion other than my sincere gratitude for Katie's help. However now and despite my ever present blisters causing discomfort Jo and I talked about more serious issues of life that had been forgotten over the previous days whilst walking with the youngsters. Jo had a friendly, kind nature and we discussed the end of life care system where she worked in a voluntary capacity and was still a raw memory for me with my parents recent passing. We then discussed our shared hobby of amateur art work, children, families, hostel living on the Camino and the magic of entering so easily into discussion with apparent strangers. After a large glass of cold Sangria on arrival at Los Arcos with Jo and Katie we were joined by Eddie once again, the Australian from Melbourne who I'd encountered previously with a large selection of Aussie jokes only surpassed by the talents of the witty Cormac from Dublin.

Cormac, who clearly spent the afternoon enjoying himself in excess, arrived in an excitable mood with a glazed expression and swaying from side to side persuaded us that he had connections with the Albergue owner where he was staying and that we were all invited for our evening meal. Sadly the disgruntled and clearly annoyed Spaniard on duty at Cormac's accommodation had no intention of allowing more diners and especially not seemingly dragged from the street! It occurred to me that the young Cormac may be on the verge of missing his own evening meal if he'd persisted with his general invitation. His Irish charm and blarney was in this instant running out! A Gluten Free Pizza was the default choice which turned out to be remarkably good and shared by the four of us outcasts enthusiastically whilst we wondered how the other Albergue diners were reacting to Cormac's particular style of humour! The following day Jo parted company from her daughter for an earlier planned departure home leaving the Camino. I suspect she was sad not to continue, she'd clearly enjoyed the experience despite some aches and pains of her own but I would lay money on her returning to continue the walk such was her obvious excitement. From a personal perspective it was sad to see her leaving for home, she had more tales to tell that would have undoubtedly been of interest to me.

BURGOS REST DAY

14961 Steps

As you can tell from today's step count there has been an unfortunate development in my Camino that will mean it will be a very different one from my previous pilgrimage nearly ten years prior. I suspected all would be well by sheer bravery, stoicism and the Camino motto of Ultreia meaning keep going but when a blister turns unpleasant and the layers of skin become infected then drastic action sadly must follow. With a fond farewell to Jack from Copenhagen, who also by coincidence needed a slight alteration and delay to his plans and a cheerful goodbye to Jo returning to England I was forced to get the bus and journey further along the Camino route. Logrono is 29 kilometres from Los Arcos and I know the decision made was for the best albeit accompanied by a sense of deep regret and a tinge of personal failure. And yet on reflection this is the Camino, this is the challenge, the uncertainty of the adventure that makes the accomplishment all the more rewarding. How naive of me to believe that my German military Meindl boots would be so comfortable and pain free as before. The exertions and training around Bewl Water on the Kent and Sussex border near where I live beforehand were one thing but the severe incline to the remote mountainside monastery of Roncesvalles on an unusually hot spring day took their toll. My slight misshapen second toe on my right foot became angry, inflamed and blistered at the challenge and so as every pilgrim knows circumstances change the dynamics.

The select group that had been formed was fun but could it be sustained for the entire length of the Camino? I suspect not and even the slightly more senior Jack had a niggling doubt that the exuberance of youth, albeit accompanied with a caring and kind nature may tire at some point of the more senior members. These youngsters especially from the United States and Canada ran half marathons, competed in cycle races, used their mobile phone devices for every request, shared information and jokes online in something called a "WhatsAPP group". Group laughter always arrived spontaneously amongst them and often proceeded the last sentence of the quip or comments making their summings up unnecessary, for those older it was clearly time consuming to explain so I often gave a friendly half smile which genuinely meant "no need to repeat on my account"!

Jack and I as senior members of the group shook hands at the bus stop whilst the youngsters headed off over the bridge rejoining the yellow signs of the Camino route. Jack was meeting his wife and also required different insoles before commencing the Way and my decision was to replace my boots in Logrono with the more trusted trekking shoes recommended by many other pilgrims on social media sites. I'm sure the youngsters would each prevail until the end with the same love of life I'd come to know and appreciate so much. Michel from Jutland Denmark who also works with adults with learning difficulties along with the departing Jack was yet another example of a well chosen career path and so fitting to his kind nature, a true gentleman. Bethany and Aparna are both destined for caring professions, indeed I seriously can't see any of this group of newly acquainted Camino pilgrims ever finding themselves taking a wrong direction in life whether socially or professionally. Daniel, a red sox baseball fan from the Boston area was the epitome and best example to have faith in the future. He had recently been working in a Polish refugee camp for displaced Ukrainians and had some sad stories to tell and yet with characteristic calm and respect didn't embellish the news as perhaps many would. He was compassionate but without being judgemental and when a solitary Swiss pilgrim at the dining table broached the issue of "Wokeism" and gender fluidity whilst

raising the interesting character of "Donald Trump" Daniel's response was to throw his head back in laughter.
"None of that bothers us, we simply don't care," was his reply. I believed Daniel's response was sincere and that's kind of the point I thought, if the young don't care about gender titles then why do those who say they are suffering at the hands of a dying breed of traditionalists with some outdated views! The future is bright, the future belongs to the young and so all those angry people who believe themselves victims of the current elderly confused generation only need to bide their time. Perhaps we should let the old traditionalists lick their confused wounds in peace!

Unfortunately and despite extensive searching in Logrono I have found no replacement boots suitable for my blistered and angry feet and even had I done so the wounded toe would need two or three days rest and so I took a bus ride to Burgos where I knew I would have more success in my searches and shopping. The journey took me through some beautiful countryside and I recognised the towns of Belorado and Santa Domingo where the live chickens clucked in the church wall and on show behind glass. The birds depict the miracle that took place in this town and as the bus passed through I reflected on my previous Camino experience and how different this pilgrimage will now be with the beginning of a second start becoming acquainted with new pilgrims. My mind wandered onto the Santa Domingo story that tells of a condemned boy who returned to life from the gallows, saved after his mother told the Judge the boy still lived whereupon the judge said that there's as much chance as this roast chicken before me being alive as your son. Sure enough the Chicken on the Judge's platter began to cluck and came back to life and the boy was immediately saved. Who am I to doubt the miracle! The story stayed with me over the years as did the scenic views and my memories strayed in dreamlike thoughts until reaching Burgos.

I'll rest again tomorrow before looking at the Cathedral, the stunning ornate inner roof that Philip II said was the nearest thing to heaven on earth prior to the failure of his Armada sent to defeat the English and spread the Catholic Word of God! Is it wrong for me to wonder momentarily how different life would be in Britain had the Spanish invasion succeeded! Perhaps the Scottish nationalists would be happy aligned with a pro EU group of Spanish influence amongst English neighbours or would they be confused further by the regions of Spain like Catalonia and the Basques where some are desperate to escape the Spanish rule. Complete imponderables but, although not remotely related to the issue of "separatism". I'm reminded of Daniel's words to the Swiss pilgrim at the meal table, "we don't really care!" Neither do I. I shake myself back to the reality of immediate issues and the search for new trekking shoes in Burgos in order to walk once more and complete my Camino. To my relief I'm successful with "On" walking shoes that bizarrely feel like carpet slippers when eased over my healing but still aching feet. I can resume my Camino escapism and dismiss all thoughts of depressing issues of politics and current affairs from home!

BURGOS REST DAY

14375 Steps

Shared meal of Sirloin Steak with Fries and Salad

A very pleasant day enjoying the Burgos sunshine with a Sangria and Vino Tinto before strolling around the city and visiting the beautiful Cathedral. Truly a special place and one that I'll visit again with my wife Kathy who expressed an interest to enter the Cathedral, stroll through the cobbled streets and enjoy the world famous Tapas. In the evening I met with Tongi who emailed me suggesting meeting for dinner saying she had moved forward along the Way as suffering from a cold. When I showed concern she suggested it could be Covid which may explain my slight sore throat over the last few days that I had dismissed as being from overcrowded dormitories with poor ventilation. The meal was exceptionally good and we discussed life and the Camino like old friends and not merely as a fine lady I'd only met just over a week before. Although I had only spent two or three days with Tongi, I liked her. Of course I did, we were pilgrims together and she told me about her successful and hard working daughter recently having graduated from her schooling, her interesting job in costume design for the film industry and her Viennese life where one day I shall visit hopefully for the New Year's Day concert! As we parted we thought we'd meet somewhere along the road on the following day towards Hornillos and I returned to my hotel knowing I'd enjoy a good night's sleep and in the knowledge that my newly acquired footwear trekking shoes would give me strength and confidence for my Camino continuance.

Rest day in Burgos

BURGOS TO SAN BOL

33419 Steps

Paella

I set off from Burgos in an excellent mood as my new shoes felt so comfortable in contrast to the heavy Meindl boots that had disappointed over the previous week or so. When I told a fellow pilgrim the retired boots, now posted home to England, are used by the German army, his reaction was to say they hadn't won many battles wearing them! In truth they've served me well and I believe they will once again but probably for a single day's hike in a day's session and not the repetitiveness of several consecutive endurance days labours. It is unusually cold in Burgos -5 degrees as I set off but I don't mind, it feels good to be setting off once again. After two hours of walking and passing many single pilgrims it became obvious that many were walking happily alone, perhaps having been in the same predicament as I and reluctantly changing their schedule. A friendly couple from Freiburg Germany, father and daughter were doing the Camino in many stages and a Mexican went past at speed only to then stop for a random Camino conversation. The reservations I had concerning meeting new groups of pilgrims and having a sense of being a loner or outsider I realised were unfounded. It was obvious that this Camino would be one of perhaps several encounters with good people.

Martin and Des, both from England, were resting outside a Cafe in the early afternoon warmth as the sun burst down upon them and it seemed a good resting place for me to join them. After a well earned ice cold fizzy orange drink I walked for what seemed a lengthy time with Martin, a retired headmaster from a school that specialises in children with special needs who are often seriously unwell. Martin mentioned the sadness of his previous job where many of the children died prematurely as a result of their health conditions. He was at a crossroads in his life with a dilemma considering whether his decision to retire was made too early or whether he'd made the right choice to leave the area where he'd lived. Martin had become semi-retired and settled in a large farmhouse in Yorkshire with his family in a possible business venture. I can relate to some of the questioning of his decision making as I'm also at a crossroads in life, as with most changes in life's circumstances I guess we all have reservations as to whether we have made the right choices. Retirement can be the most rewarding and fun period with exciting possibilities but it can also give a daunting glimpse of the future that inevitably will include issues of poor health and a loss of purpose. For my part as an underachiever retirement brings an end to the fantasy prospect that something magical might materialise, that something might rekindle a love of life that only the youth truly appreciate who aren't troubled by aches or pains and thoughts of mortality and the as yet not experienced sense of disappointment being undervalued or overlooked for promotion within the workplace. Martin felt confident that his journey on the Way would answer his dilemmas and questioning but I suspect like me that only an acceptance of life as it is now will give him the answer. I later found Martin was awarded an honour for his work as a head teacher and so I can imagine his decision to change direction must have been a brave and momentous one. In his case he made his mark as an achiever and proudly should be congratulated with a feeling of self worth and contentment, in my case I was too lazy but the moment has passed to feel the sense of achievement that Martin once had and I will never know! We parted company at Hornilos but I hope to meet him again.

After walking through two remote and isolated villages there was Tongi sitting on a street bench enjoying the warm sunshine.
"Hello Richard, there's no beds at the next stage so I've booked two

beds in a dormitory at San Bol."

I didn't mind, my Camino attitude and approach, as with the one previously, is quite happy to be led by those with their greater experience and judgement which is now even more relevant in the age of clever Apps. The Albergue chosen by Tongi at San Bol sits nestled between two hills of rolling green barley and has a stream running through that is said to deliver miracle treatment to weary pilgrims and their aching feet. My brother Chris has stayed here before and indeed said it is magical, I can imagine in the hotter summer months it really is a special experience as the icy water runs into a purpose built bath before flowing down a slope adjacent to the accommodation. The Camino has provided another enchanting experience, this time of peaceful tranquillity and intimacy with a dormitory of just twelve beds but with only three occupants. Tongi and I are joined later by just one other pilgrim, Barbara from Sweden and therefore we can expect a good sleep.

The Albergue Hospitalario was a young Spanish lady who explained that she lived nearby but not on site, she said how we should lock up and leave the key safely squirrelled away the following morning and then asked if we required the evening communal meal which would be a Paella, my first in Spain. It promised to be a wonderful evening with just three pilgrims and ample portions of the Spanish national dish accompanied by their fine wine. I sat for a lengthy period soaking my feet in the icy waters next to Tongi who was doing the same and chatted with Barbara who was by now hanging her clothes to dry before us. We were all hungry and so in turn made our way eventually to the dining area next to the small galley kitchen. Sadly the illicium paradise of the location came to an end as we each saw the Paella on the stove that consisted of three small chicken legs and yellow rice without any of the other ingredients that one would expect to find in a Paella!

SAN BOL TO BOADILLA DEL CAMINO

47564 Steps

Roast Chicken and Chips

I left the San Bol small Albergue where I'd spent the night with Tongi and the later arrival, a Swedish nomadic hippie with a friendly kind nature, what Boris Johnson our late prime minister, might call a "crusty" in the nicest sense of the phrase. Barbara was a very easy going and relaxed lady with a gentle tone and spoke perfect English. I recall affectionately her singing of Swedish lullabies which were charming and well meant as we drifted off to sleep after the evening meal. The morning was very cold as usual but the sky was blue, the birds sang and the cool morning air was just right for the fast pace I set before Tongi and Barbara caught up with me at Castrojeriz where I'd stopped for the morning coffee and the first break of the day. Tongi who is light in frame and fit walked faster from this point on than Barbara and I and was therefore soon walking ahead leaving Barbara and I to discuss her interesting lifestyle in Sweden. She lived with her husband on a small holding and made a living with a few livestock supplemented by the making of cutlery and kitchen utensils made from wood felled off their land. She used her garden Sauna daily and painted a picture of domestic bliss in the remote idyll of her rural farm when not travelling away and spending her holidays walking the Camino or bizarrely camping in her small car along with her husband for long periods. Barbara was another example of the typical Camino pilgrim I encountered with a very kind nature. She is active in the charity work of migrants moving to Sweden from Middle East countries which inevitably lead our conversation towards the cultural differences and the need for those either moving to or those welcoming to adapt!

Tongi, Barbara and I had previously decided on where we would sleep this evening and over the breakfast coffee it was further agreed but on arrival and having so easily walked for the first twenty kilometres of the day we opted for a section further and the next village with a municipal Albergue. This was a huge mistake, it was closed without reason or explanation as was the following one which added in my case for a lengthy and annoying diversion as a sign post suggested another nearby hostel. Tongi and Barbara continued on the official path whilst I went in search of the illusive accommodation. I enjoy the Camino experience but the daily challenge of my planned walk is a sufficient test for my endurance, character and level of fitness. When this changes for unexpected reasons like Albergue closures it is extremely frustrating. I prayed that I would find a bed, any bed, sheltering behind a straw bale with wild animals and bugs were fearful thoughts that kept coming to my mind and leading to the prospect of me considering a taxi to the nearest town before a rapid return to England. By this point I was tired, hot, frustrated and annoyed. Tongi was now somewhere ahead, after my detour, following the yellow arrows and scallop signs, she may have had some success with her booking App unlike me but it was the Swedish hippie Barbara that I felt most sorry for who like me is from an older age group and perhaps less familiar with booking Apps and a lady possibly now walking alone. I thought she may find herself knocking on a stranger's front door and asking or begging for assistance somewhere behind me down the Camino route.

I'm blessed. Truly I am, the small town of Boadilla del Camino came into sight with the church tower growing nearer with each lonely and laboured step I made as most fellow pilgrims would by now have arrived at their destinations. On arrival I got one of the last beds in the attic dormitory of twenty plus beds. The hostel was part of a hotel accommodation and was clean with marble floors and all the modern required amenities. I would have paid a thousand pounds for a bed or whatever was asked of me in my state of tired anguish.

After a much needed shower I chatted with Anne in the very late afternoon sun in the communal garden, a nurse and data analyst from the Republic of Ireland and at dinner I sat next to Eva from Prague and opposite Olivier from Provence who are two more shining examples of youthfulness on Camino and enjoying life. We drank the local wine and ate the fine roast chicken dinner, little did I know that Eva and Olivier would feature again on my later Camino but I would lose touch completely with Anne. The conversation was largely centred around our good fortune that we had found this oasis after the difficulties that we had all experienced looking for accommodation over the latter part of the day's walk.

In the huge dormitory I spoke with John from Donnegal, an amiable and pleasant chap who, against all recommended advice, may walk the long day tomorrow across the seventeen kilometres of Maseta where there is no shelter, drinking water or amenities. After the day's walk I'd just undertaken I had no intention of walking this risky distance without shelter despite it being early in the year and therefore avoiding the Spanish heat in the height of summer. I decided to stick with Eva and Oliver walking a mere twenty five kilometres and stopping just shy of the long slog that would be enjoyed on the following day. Today has taught me not to overdo it and perhaps my accompanying Tongi might not have been a good idea as she regularly and successfully overstepped the recommended stages suggested by the guide books and APPs. That said, I have a bed and perhaps she doesn't but there again, I am blessed!

Crossing the Meseta

BOADILLA DEL CAMINO TO CARRIÓN DE LOS CONDE

34642 Steps

Packet of nuts, cereal bar

An interesting walk out of Boadilla del Camino as I said goodbye to the exceptionally kind manager with a Rastopharian hairstyle who had been my welcoming saviour from the day before with not just my acceptance but a complimentary washing of clothes. I suspect he saw the relief on my face on arrival! I was buoyed by a good night's sleep and made my way in the fresh air to the canal and towards Fromista. After a while with the sun rising I removed my jacket and whilst pushing it down into my bulging rucksack a voice called out.
"Good morning Richard."
I recognised it as that of the friendly Tongi walking at a fast pace from behind and on her way also to Fromista, unlike me she was destined for the train station and from there to Leon. She wished to skip the section ahead in order to allow more time to enjoy the more scenic part of the Camino in Galicia. Apparently she and Barbara had slept at someone's house that sounded from her description to be nothing more than a room over a convenience store. I made the right noises and was glad that she and Barbara had found a resting place but deep down knew my evening and the liberal friendly hospitality that I enjoyed would have been the better choice for them also.

I said my goodbyes to Tongi but suspect I haven't seen the last of her yet, I can envisage being in Santiago de Compostela and a voice calling out from behind me! We exchanged emails and with the promise to send photographs from Santiago de Compostela

Tongi disappeared into the train station as I walked on. Sadly her moving ahead so far along the Camino meant that we wouldn't meet again but we did share photographs of delight on our completions.

After Fromista I met up with John from Ireland on the lengthy and at times monotonous straight road towards Carrion de las Conde. John was a likeable man who like me doesn't necessarily believe all he is told by the media but his conspiracy theories became a tad odd and perhaps absurd especially when the subject of 9/11 inevitably was raised in the context of his views on the United States. As John had discussed with me the evening before he was setting off on the seventeen kilometres ahead across the barren Maseta when we parted company despite the repeated warnings that the pilgrims should go armed with lots of drinking water and most importantly with fresh legs. A brave but perhaps foolhardy decision I thought after the length of the distance already walked this day but the time went quickly walking with John and so I'll miss his witty and bizarre beliefs.

As John departed I met Allan in Carrion de Las Conde, another Irish man who laughs at my jokes regardless of their amusing content or not. Allan was down to earth and unlike his fellow countryman, who we watched walking away, was completely uninterested in Brexit or any other issue unrelated to the escapism of the Camino. Tomorrow Allan has decided to walk two full stages of the Brierly guidebook and trek for fifty kilometres whereas I shall walk a mere twenty and seek some more relaxed fun. Allan was of more senior age like myself and was keen to meet up with his wife at Sarria so this perhaps explains his understandable urgency but he had the good sense to send his backpack on by the courier service that is widely available on the route and probably a good idea for those with injuries related to the wearing of a rucksack or walking exceptionally long distances. He looked to be merely a local in a hurry when I last saw him.

CARRIÓN DE LOS CONDE TO MORATINOS

38523 Steps

Soup, Chicken and Chips, Ice cream

Today was a terrific day and one I won't forget in a hurry. I left the Convent where I'd spent the night and before departing decided on the breakfast kindly offered the day before. The eighty one year old nun refused any money or donation offered by me and gave me a lavish spread of toast, cake , coffee and fresh fruit. I shared the table with two Germans from Hamburg and Stutgart who occasionally broke into pigeon English to be sociable. Setting off, the nun gave me a warm smile, stroked my arm with a blessing and wished me a truly heartfelt "Buen Camino". Her very expression lifted the soul and the walk out of Carrion de Los Condes was crisp, cold and uplifting of spirit. I passed a few pilgrims in discussion wishing them well until I came across Carmel, a retired physiotherapist from Sydney Australia. We chatted about Camino life, current affairs, the questions of a religious calling to walk the Way of St James until the inevitable discussion arises between an Aussie and an Englishman whether it be in a foreign land or either of our home countries. No, not our shared Royal family, nor the selfish antics or not of Prince Harry and Megan Markle that we would laugh about later! Our attention turned to the passion of Ashes cricket and we spent over twenty kilometres discussing current and former players over the last forty years, details of Ashes series and the sad demise of the legendary Australian great spin bowler Shane Warne.

We arrived having crossed the longest stretch of the Maseta where there is the lack of amenities that I previously mentioned and reached a picturesque town where I drank water and a single glass of cold wine to recharge the batteries along with bananas and an energy bar. Here I was introduced by Carmel to Amanda, a PE teacher and ex professional squash player from Perth Australia of similar age to myself but much fitter and with an obvious love of life. Rarely in this world do you meet a character such as Amanda, within just a half hour of conversation she left a lasting impression of a vivacious love of all things. She had a sparkle and twinkle in the eye and of course she loved cricket. We chatted for what seemed like only moments with the subject ranging from Denis Lillee's bowling action and style to the famous Ashes series of 2005 and ending the chat with the heavenly presence of God seen in the pilgrims crossing the Way. Despite the temptation to remain with Amanda and the pilgrims at this village my mind was set on moving on for the full stage of the day and so Carmel and I headed off towards the next town. Amanda's demeanour was infectious, the crucifix around her neck accompanied by the necklace of Mary told me her journey was spiritual but I was left with a feeling that had I not walked on I may have finished the Way with her and found the subsequent parting a deep wrench as is the case with long friendships made along the Camino.

The John Brierly guide suggested a stage ending at a desperately depressing point therefore Carmel and I walked on until reaching Moratinos where we were joined in the hostel by a Canadian named Jack who had the appearance of a vagrant. I can't work out whether he's a tramp or an eccentric. Another Canadian gentleman named Jean Claud was staying in a private room at the adjacent hotel who was a French speaker from Quebec and I wondered in the moment whether there would be an interesting difference between the two Canadians. Why would there be with them both being good Pilgrims on the Way I told myself but my intuition was correct as they didn't greet each other in the manner that fellow kinsmen would on foreign shores. Jack didn't dine with us being a vegetarian, he didn't accept my offer of a drink being a non drinker and something felt instinctively odd.

But who am I to judge the Camino way where the unexpected keeps delivering daily surprises. Who would have thought I'd spend a day walking across a hot dusty Spanish plain talking to Australians about cricket and I'll never forget the experience.

Hontanas on a hot day

MORITANOS TO BERCIANOS DEL REAL

28634 Steps

Beef Burger

Jack from Canada was the first to set off in complete darkness from Moratinos but not before he had chatted with Carmel and I about his chosen route that might deviate away from the well marked path. He liked the quiet solitude and I soon realised that I had completely misjudged him because of his shyness and it struck me the stupidity of my first impressions related to his vagrant-like appearance. I think there is a possibility that he lives on the Camino which may explain his dishevelled look, we shook hands warmly and he was gone leaving me not merely to question my premature judgement but to feel a small degree of shame. Immediately before Carmel departed we walked together up the steep grassy knoll opposite our Albergue that was a man made and now disused housing for Spanish folks in a bygone era. Small entrances with metal bars were dug into the mound and used as storage areas now for discarded rubbish and old farm equipment along with evidence of wine once there. The views from the top and the rising sun made a spectacular vista of the flat Spanish countryside of where we had come from and in the opposite direction where we would be walking today. I embraced Carmel warmly but to my surprise within the hour I had once again caught up with her which was a pleasing sight after our varied and friendly conversation from the previous day. We spoke freely once more and the walk was bracing with views of the mountains in the distance to our right, the corn fields blowing in the wind and the turbines turning gently on our left.

Carmel and I entered a Cafe on the outskirts of Sahagun for breakfast and enjoyed a warm potato omelette that is served widely in Spain and suits my gluten intolerance diet unlike the excess of pastries however appealing they may be. Carmel told me about her intended house move from her apartment in Sydney to the Blue Mountains nearby in Australia. It looked idyllic as she shared her mobile phone pictures. I liked Carmel, she had some traditional views like me but when discussing further it became obvious that she spoke in certainties on some issues that slightly puzzled me. I can understand one describing themselves as an agnostic, although I am a believer, but not as an atheist as you can't have faith that something isn't true! Carmel said she was a nonbeliever and added further assertions on wider issues for instance that climate change is a made up cult bordering on a new religion. I laughed saying I really don't know but we both agreed that Greta Thurnberg would be better enjoying life as would all the crusty types glueing themselves to motorway tarmac and creating havoc for innocent passers by! Carmel and I both like Donald Trump, for me simply as entertainment value and a cartoon character but she has a belief and support for some of his policies whereas I have serious doubts. Again we laughed and it was clear that the conversations ran smoothly between us, how toxic the former president is in conversation with so many and indeed as is the issue of climate change that it simply can't be discussed as too controversial within some social circles. Once again, and at this point of my Camino, I found controversial subjects can be freely addressed at least amongst those like Carmel without leading to the awkwardness that they perhaps would away from the pilgrimage experience. Carmel was destined for a change of her Camino route travelling to the Norte section that hugs the north coastline of Spain. We embraced for the second time and I reminded her that the undulating Norte route is tough on the legs but she grinned, I think her outdoor lifestyle "down under" will outweigh any discomfort in her labours and the scenery is supposedly stunning. She had planned to undertake two weeks of voluntary work in the English hostel on the Norte that is run by the Confraternity of St James before finishing her walk, a later email exchange with Carmel said that she found the voluntary work very rewarding and enjoyable.

Further into Sahagun sat Piere Henri, Olivier and Eva at a Cafe and I paused for a conversation about their Way since my last meeting with them, we were four foreigners together each different from the other and freely in conversation having met not two days prior but now joined by the Camino spirit of friendship. It being Easter Sunday the town square was packed with families enjoying the early sunshine and awaiting the procession of the life size figures of the Virgin Mary and Christ raised into the air by those chosen from the town and accompanied by a brass band. I sat drinking cold Galician Albarino wine with Jean Claude from Quebec who I'd met from the previous evening and instantly formed a liking for. We both agreed and found the Easter celebration spectacle very moving, respectful and full of admiration for the tradition and yet at times it felt a bit more like a sombre solemn Good Friday procession than the Easter Sunday celebrations that we both knew and loved from our childhood memories that centred around the excesses of chocolate and other treats.

Over a couple of further white wines we discussed wider issues such as the Covid pandemic where we both agreed that if God was responsible for nature and if nature occasionally sends pandemics to cull the weak in the population then how stupid to fight against nature and find a vaccine. Only the traditional use of isolation should be used to control its spread accompanied by the power of prayer and the miracles widely known in folklore that ensue. Perhaps the wine was working its magic too well in the company of Jean Claude and we found ourselves laughing at these Covid issues that worked the masses into a frenzy and apparently still do! It was ironic Jean Claud said that he worked in an old people's home during Covid in order to save lives, the very opposite of the hard and maybe cynical views we'd just discussed. I hope to meet

Jean Claude again later on the Way but he'd had foot injuries that would delay his walk over the next two days with the need to rest.

The journey from Sahagun took me through the town and into the countryside where I bumped into Jorge from Stutgart and then Walter from Switzerland before reaching Berricarlos. Another good day on the Camino and a memorable Easter Sunday.

BERCIANOS DEL REAL TO LEON

43642 Steps

Hamburger & Vino Tinto

A really long day but this time I have a hotel booked for two nights with a rest day to look around the City of Leon and so my heart and spirits are lifted despite the tiresome final walk into the outskirts of the lively and vibrant city. The morning started as usual with me deep in contemplative thought as I always am for the first two hours of the stroll that sees the sun rise and the crisp cold air turn to warmth as one peels the layers of clothing off every half hour or so. Each item bedded down with a degree of pressure into the rucksack and the realisation that despite the extra comfort in removing items the load on your back is growing in weight.

The walk is flat and monotonous on this section but the ensuite Hotel room is calling me on and I periodically bump into Camino friends from before but mostly newer faces. Firstly, an extremely fit New Zealander and then soon followed by an Irish man who states he is keen to keep walking for a full day in order to prevent an early arrival where there is a temptation to pat oneself on the back and then overindulge in the pleasure of copious amounts of beer and wine. I can relate to this sensation as on arrival and after a shower the communal garden is a terrific setting for putting one's feet up and enjoying a beer or two which can easily lead to more on the pretext that you are deserving after walking a long distance. Another reason for a quickening pace could be from a competitive nature as the office in Santiago de Compostela now offers a second certificate registering the time one has taken to complete the Camino. I'm not sure what my reasoning is for a quickening pace today other than on this particular stretch the scenery isn't noteworthy but mainly my reasoning is from a guilty perspective of pleasure as I contemplate yet again the hotel room with the possibility of a bath and a certain night of comfort.

On arrival in Leon I met Christian, a Danish Camino friend that I first encountered after Pamplona and up until Estella, who looked to be wandering in a lonely fashion near the Cathedral. Christian has an aura of gentleness, kindness and dare I say it from a heterosexual point of view he is extremely good looking. He has piercing blue eyes and neoclassical statuesque features with an olive tanned complexion and unblemished skin. I suspect many would welcome his company from all demographics and walks of society but on this encounter he was clearly downhearted. He had sad news from home having been informed of the death of his grandmother who he was close to, he had travelled ahead by public transport on his Camino with a foot problem and appeared to be keen to chat over a wine having been forcibly separated from his Camino group that many of whom were known to me. I was extremely tired from the many days of long walking and wanted nothing more than a bath and a long sleep but despite this Christian's need for company was obvious and therefore we shared a bottle of Vino Tinto followed by a Hamburger each eaten alfresco with the floodlit beautiful Cathedral as our backdrop. We parted company with a Camino embrace and Christian decided to walk once more on the following day, now with the need to complete the distance quickly before returning for the family funeral back in Denmark.

A rest day in Leon was greatly appreciated, much needed and inspirational. I woke fresh and healed from the previous many tiring days and after a hotel breakfast took the tour of the Cathedral as I had done nearly ten years prior. This time I was more attentive to the details with my audio tour downloaded onto my mobile phone device, perhaps the Camino was helping me with my use of technology failings. The mediaeval stained glass in the Cathedral is stunning with amazing vivid colours and the history of its building and subsequent saving from crumbling stonework is a fascinating tale. After the tour I sat aghast at the sights on an isolated pew and felt a heavenly presence about me! Was it the sensation caused by my position where there was a contrast of cooler air against the huge thick stone walls that moved me, was it a glimpse of a statue or icon of significance nearby, could it be a memory brought to life by a sense of smell! Maybe, who can say but it could be something deeper, something spiritually present that touched me in the moment. I left the Cathedral into the warm summer sunshine renewed in my determination to walk on. The ancient Camino word used by pilgrims over the centuries came to my mind once more, Utereia meaning "keep going" and tomorrow I will.

Leon cathedral at night

LEON TO VILLAR DE MAZARIFE

27847 Steps

Leaving Leon was depressing for two reasons, firstly because it was sad to leave such a beautiful city where I appreciated the culture, history and atmosphere left by years of passing and excited pilgrims in and around the Cathedral, the cobbled streets and inside the walled city area. Secondly, the industrial scenery on the outskirts of the city is truly awful in contrast to the magic from within and therefore I found the experience especially grim. Stopping for a coffee in the next town I was heartened by the arrival of Eva who I'd last seen in Sahagun and she stopped joining me for a coffee as is the friendly Camino manner and we entered into a discussion about the Cathedral in Leon, marriage and her possible upcoming trip to New Zealand which is next on her exciting list of carefree travel around the globe. She was keen to walk on alone having allowed Olivier to walk on before her, she jokingly likened the time she had spent walking with Olivier from France to a form of marriage. I knew what she meant as the Camino has a habit of allowing pilgrims to become familiar in an amazing short period of time and yet there are periods where solo contemplation is required.

I walked on and the scenery eventually improved. The snow on the northern mountains to my right and in the distance was still there and the carpet of bright green crops in the wide fields rustled in the wind with the propeller blades of turbines still gently turning occasionally in unison. Ahead of me in the distance was a pilgrim with a similar pace and speed and therefore it took a long while before the distance between us gradually grew closer. Would it be a South Korean, Japanese or Asian walker who may be less likely to enter into an English conversation I wondered? The view of a fellow pilgrim as you approach from behind gives you a strange intuitive sense of their country of origin. Some bizarrely carry a national flag draped down from their rucksack, others a smaller flag on a stick and as one grows nearer some boast proudly their nationality with a badge stitched into their backpack. If these obvious signs are missing something instinctively tells you where they might be domiciled without seeing any clues. Sure enough I was right with my guess that this pilgrim was from the United States, perhaps it was the expensive rucksack and well known branded trekking clothing but the friendly pronunciation of "Buen Camino" gave away the final clue. It was Timothy James (TJ) from Seattle who had an interesting story to tell, he'd worked for fifteen years in Budapest setting up a software company from its infancy. TJ, like many others I'd met, was kind, sociable and friendly and we reached the municipal Albergue in good time with the opportunity of washing clothes in a long drying period of afternoon sun.

TJ and I were settled on the lawn where we were joined by Muk, a young vivacious and attractive girl from a small village north of Amsterdam Netherlands, she has an incredible understanding of English and the ability to allow people bizarrely to open up about their inner feelings and the three of us spent four hours in the sunny garden chatting about everything ranging from the temptations of materialism to food allergies in the young and old. Nothing was off topic in discussion with this young Dutch girl as is the Camino spirit but I'm still grounded enough with my reserved nature and mixed with a sense of discipline to know that there are still parameters and boundaries that ought not to be crossed especially accompanied with free flowing Spanish wine. I can't be sure whether walking the Way with this Dutch girl would be enthralling or perhaps have an element of risk that might distract my focus as I remind myself that the Camino for me is an enjoyable endurance and challenge of mind and body but not a holiday. I suspect that tomorrow we'll part company on the Way walking at a different pace but I'd like to meet up socially again, near or at Santiago de Compostela and indeed with Eva, Olivier and the recently encountered TJ who are now in jocular mood by my side basking in the Camino Spanish sunshine.

The evening entertainment continued in the same vein of Camino fun but I had serious doubts as to the chicken dinner which I suspected might be rabbit and I looked for confirmation from TJ who grinned knowingly at my suggestions. Very small odd pieces of grey looking boney meat were on the plates before us. It was accompanied by the usual liberal hospitality of Vino Tinto and followed with a "digestive" drink suggested by TJ, a lemon coloured herbal drink from Spain. Olivier, a vegetarian, cooked a separate pasta dish in the communal kitchen and for once I was quite envious of his lifestyle choice as I reflected along with TJ at what we may have just eaten.

It was another enjoyable day and although this is the most basic of hostels I've stayed in yet with cracked tiles in the shower and bathrooms, dodgy and possibly dangerous looking electrical wiring, loose bannister rails and overcrowding the ambiance and instinctive appeal was alluring. The bar area was full of scruffy local farming peasants shouting at each other from close range and the final scene as I climbed the rickety stairs gingerly to bed was of a live chicken being plunged into a sack by one of the locals. Perhaps the accompanying laughter from the drinkers was in the knowledge that the Chicken menu pilgrim dish of the day was safely being carried out of the door and that the substituted rabbit had seemingly been eaten undetected! The luxury of my hotel in Leon is now a distant memory!

VILLAR DE MAZARIFE TO ASTORGA

42387 Steps

Vegetarian meal with Dutch and French pilgrims

I left Villa de la Mazariff in the extreme cold and walked for what seemed a long while before seeing a sign stating that I'd only covered a measly four kilometres of distance. The wind was blowing strongly and I wished I'd packed warm winter gloves from home but in truth there is no spare room or further capacity in my rucksack. After my first coffee break of the day, having walked a good ten kilometres, I saw the familiar figure of Olivier from Provence France accompanied by the sound of each of his walking poles hitting the tarmac road that gave away his identity long before I reached his side. Olivier is a very interesting man to speak with as he has many hidden depths and talents, not least his fascinating lifestyle where he visits India to teach the art of meditation revived some seventy years ago but dating back to pre Christianity and the teachings of Buddha. Olivier informed me that the meditation lasts a full eleven days where those assembled aren't allowed any distractions or to make eye contact with each other. I would be highly sceptical of these eleven days of silent meditation if it were not for meeting Olivier whose calm and quiet demeanour and character I think would be suited to this lifestyle, he had an inner peace that is rarely seen in others. Ironically I met other pilgrims later on this Camino who also said they had practised the same art of meditation for the full eleven days and my initial reaction was to laugh albeit without showing, one of the characters had a nature that was the polar opposite of the calmness that Olivier exuded. My later experiences of walking with Olivier would highlight his calmness under stress as opposed to my more frustrated and perhaps when compared intolerant disposition.

It was a long tiring day, despite the enjoyment of walking with Olivier and at times Eva, as we entered Astorga and therefore we declined a trip suggested by other pilgrims to visit the Gaudi museum and settled instead for a cold drink in one of the bars in the scenic town square. In truth I don't particularly appreciate Gaudi's style of architecture which to me is reminiscent of Disneyland attractions and so it wasn't a difficult decision to make swapping instead for the atmospheric cobbled square meeting point beneath the town hall clock and in sight of the plaster figures that come out to chime the bells. In the municipal Albergue and sharing the six bedded room with me is another pilgrim with a powerful presence, a highly intelligent young woman from Amsterdam named Julia who is employed by a Dutch bank to encourage and investigate the ethical side of banking and with a second job teaching Philosophy. She is fun, grounded and appealing in nature with a strong and confident sense and inner belief that with her chosen career profession she can make a difference and encourage the people in power to change their ways resulting in a fairer society. Old age and cynicism has left me sceptical but it's truly wonderful to see the enthusiasm and optimism in Julia, the very fact she is employed in a banking position to make the needed change perhaps indicates that mindsets are indeed improving unless it's merely a corporate publicity stunt!

We spent the evening with a communal vegetarian meal cooked by Olivier, Julia and Pierre Henri and afterwards I shared Camino photos from my experiences so far with Martine from Cologne. She and I had both started from St Jean Pied de Port just three days apart and therefore knew some fellow pilgrims from the earlier stages and this showed me that my injury induced skipping of a slight stage before Burgos hadn't made a tremendous difference to the ultimate appreciation of my Camino experience. I also met Martha from Zurich Switzerland who with the aid of her Swiss Army knife allowed me to offer another bottle of Vino Tinto for enjoyment. This was another tiring Camino day with a heavy step count but still very rewarding and the vital reassurance needed that if you find yourself amongst a new gathering of pilgrims, many of those around me freshly starting out from Astorga, it doesn't take long to feel at ease and comfortable once more amongst newly met walkers that were strangers moments before. From my sleeping bag I reflected on the day whilst sinking into a deep sleep and I considered Olivier's vegetarian and bohemian lifestyle but whilst tempted by the relaxed and peaceful state I'm not a convert to the Buddhist meditation he follows. I'm still here for St James the Apostle amongst other more enjoyable earthly matters and rewarding pleasures.

The view from the Albergue at Astorga

ASTORGA TO RABANAL DEL CAMINO

25488 Steps

Nuts and Fruit

An extremely difficult and grim walk due to the weather conditions, who would have thought that within a day of leaving the long walking stretch across the northern dry Maseta of Spain in April I would experience not just low temperatures of -2 degrees but now accompanied by driving winds, sleet and snow! How I wished I'd delayed my Camino by a further month but this may have taken me into the more extreme walking conditions of excessive heat. Therefore with my rain Jacket hood up and covering as best I could my raw face I focussed merely on each step of the path before me and despite this being a much shorter stretch than I had become accustomed to over the last few weeks it was tough going.

On reaching Rabanal del Camino I was advised that the English run Albergue that I had intended to use was closed, however I called at the door regardless as I'm a member of the Confraternity of St James that has its headquarters in Blackfriars London. I was greeted by Fiona who then introduced me to the other volunteers Ray and Anne who were exceptionally kind, offering me late afternoon Yorkshire tea and homemade gluten free flapjack. Sadly they had received a visit from the local Mayor who had ordered them to close the doors to all visitors with a scare of arsenic poisoning in the local water. I later found that the municipal Albergue hadn't warned Olivier and Eva who had spent the night there about any dangers to the drinking water and therefore the problem must have been very localised! Fiona, Ray and Anne chatted to me for around two hours about social niceties and our lives in England, their volunteering here in Spain and Fiona's passion for the Portuguese Camino that starts from Lisbon but becomes very picturesque as it divides into three scenic routes from Porto. Definitely on my list of future adventures and if starting from Porto with just eleven days of walking one that I may encourage my wife Kathy to enjoy also. I was invited back for breakfast by Fiona the following morning and I agreed without hesitation knowing that the hot porridge would be very welcome especially as the weather forecast was for another bitterly cold morning.

I stayed in a private room with an ensuite for some much needed extra sleep and the privacy of an en-suite shower and more personal amenities but having been given a guided tour of the English hostel by Ray and its clean well appointed beds I instinctively felt the English friendly environment would have suited me better had it not been for the Arsenic in the water! The pension hotel host suggested some Gregorian chanting in the local church which I had intended to visit were it not for another heavy downpour of rain coinciding with my leaving the front door and having already been soaked throughout the day I soon altered my plans and returned to the comfort of my room. A small mounted portable television in the room showed a football match between Feyenoord against Roma which was good background entertainment as I wrote some notes for this journal. I'm contemplating having a shave in this private room of hedonism away from the Camino lifestyle that I've almost become accustomed to but will I feel any less of a pilgrim when clean shaven?

RABANAL DEL CAMINO TO MOLINASECA

341199 Steps

Tortilla and vegetarian food

The day started so well with an invite from the English managed Albergue for a porridge breakfast kindly prepared by Fiona, one of the Hospitalario volunteers who along with Ray and Anne didn't notice my clean shaven face from the previous afternoon. Such generosity is incredible to a stranger and I am heartened by the attractive setting of Rabanal del Camino and the small church opposite where my wonderful fellow countrymen and women offer support and encouragement. However this is where my good fortune and any good humour or enjoyment came to an abrupt end as I entered something akin to the film movie set of 'The Perfect Storm' starring George Clooney where he stars on a small stricken fishing vessel. Torrential and continual rain, sleet and snow lashed my body accompanied by strong gale force winds so that after four kilometres of walking and reaching Foncebaden there was little point in stopping having been completely drenched and soaked with no sign of a change in the weather. Everything was sodden to the core and my only comfort was a wrapped but now soggy helping of gluten free flapjack given by Fiona prior to my departure from Rabanal del Camino. Would that I hadn't left!

This should have been the highlight of the Camino pilgrimage with the Cruz de Farer Cross of great significance being the highest section of the entire Camino walk and the inspirational highlight of the whole month's endeavours. All I could do was bow my head briefly as I passed and looked on at the tall wooden cross that is surrounded by small stones left from all corners of the world by passing pilgrims. There was no chance of personal reflection with me battling the elements and being battered by the driving wind and rain like the said George Clooney trying to steer his sinking vessel. Eventually I made it to the next village and stumbled through the doorway of a cafe bar in a bad and disgruntled mood desperate on this occasion for some shelter but realising it would come at the cost of purchasing coffee and further orders to justify the hour or more needed to stay out of the "perfect storm" and indoors. Eventually after peeling off three layers of drenched clothing, that when piled on the wooden floorboards left a spreading puddle, supposedly made to protect from the fierce downpours my waterproof wallet and pilgrim passport came into sight. My Euro banknotes and card passport were on the point of mulching into oblivion before my eyes into a paper mache dollop on the floor beside the watery splash I'd left from now discarded clothing. Fortunately the café owner was happy to take the wet ten euro bank note that was just about still intact and bring the much needed hot Cafe con leche to my table and seat.

Here my luck changed for the better, how could it get any worse! After drying for an hour I started a conversation with Anne Milner, an Irish lady living in England, proudly wearing a large crucifix around her neck who seemingly spends most of her time on walking pilgrimages. She told me about her many walks and one in particular heading to Jerusalem in the Holy land only to be prevented and halted by the war in Syria. A strong dose and sense of realism struck me, how could I complain about the rain in the morning when talking to this fine lady who offered me a blessing when I left the shelter of the cafe later. God, who I had asked, when likening my experiences to that of George Clooney who was in a state of mortal danger, stopped the torrential rain and wind and the descent into Molinaseca was the needed contrast to reassure me that life is still good and a hint of a rainbow gave further proof of God's promise that He would never flood the earth again!

Walking over the stone mediaeval bridge I saw my French friend Olivier along with Eva paddling in the rapidly moving waters of the river below and after a Lemon flavoured local beer, a Spanish delight I'd become keen on, we booked into a hostel where we used the communal washing machine, one wash for our combined load. We walked through the attractive street's of Molinaseca as the warm evening sun burst through and purchased wine and vegetables for the evening dinner, leaving them back in the hostel before wondering out once again where I met for the first time the colourful and friendly Australian pilgrims Cheryl, Sue and Nick. An hour passed quickly as we each reflected on the experience of the day's walking and whilst being annoyed when missing the pleasure of the walk that passed the Cross in the wet we all agreed that this was a good way to end the day.

On returning to the hostel the host and owner had bizarrely emptied the washing machine and presumably used another setting to dry the clothes which brought a raised eyebrow from Olivier and me and clear annoyance from Eva who said she didn't want her clothing or undergarments handled by a stranger. It was disconcerting indeed and certainly not what one would expect from hostel Albergue living where such things are done solely by the backpackers. It was also annoying to see my bottle of red wine open on the table albeit still full and the cork nestling on the rim of the bottle. Clearly the host is either over intrusive in his actions or exceptionally kind depending on your point of view!

Other pilgrims arrived, an Englishman from Somerset covered in tattoos and wild long black tangled hair named Oliver and a girl named Eliia from Moscow Russia who had worked and knew very well the area of Kent where I live. All in all it had been an incredible and interesting day of contrasting moods and emotions, the cruel severe weather spoiled the highlight of the day's walk and left me on the verge of giving up the whole venture and heading for home. To many who may read this account you may think I'm exaggerating the weather conditions that we faced today but

I can't state enough the severity of the cold or piercing sleet that I and other pilgrims had endured! However my discussion with Anne who walked pilgrimages in really dangerous war torn conditions and not just extremely bad weather made me realise how childish I was in my overly annoyed attitude. Her example and the pleasant ending of the day and evening was sufficient for me to laugh with the other previously sodden pilgrims and relish the following day's walk with a better forecast. The sad fate and ending of the George Clooney film, that I compared our pilgrimage ordeal to, with his demise along with the fishing boat crew was a laughable over exaggeration that saw the English Oliver laugh loudly. I suspect the other pilgrims hadn't seen the movie and therefore missed the humour!

MOLINASECA TO VILLAFRANCA

39996 Steps

Awful Soup, dreadful Tortilla and Tin fruit!

As Olivier, Eva and I descended the stairs of the Albergue we found our shoes laid out on the steps with individual shoe horns provided adjacent to each pair and a free postcard of the hostel placed against the outer right side shoe. Surely this level of service wouldn't be provided by the most expensive and upmarket hotel and Olivier and I both considered that we may have misjudged the genial and kind host who had also put my sodden and almost ruined pilgrim passport in the bakery shop oven that he owned next to the hostel and in doing so saved it and my whole further Camino. The Albergues can't be used or visited without the pilgrim passport and the Compostela not issued without the stamped evidence of each night's travel. The host may have been eccentric but there can be no doubt his efforts were genuine and heartfelt. Eva, Olivier and I walked away from the hostel saying goodbye to Eliia the Muscovite girl who left a profound and lasting impression on me, not least because I've been fed the one sided news from the British media for so long that it's easy to wrongly fall into the trap of believing that every Russian is evil! I would get to know Eliia further as my Camino continued.

A truly wonderful day followed in contrast to the weather conditions of the day before, bright blue skies with the occasional aeroplane trails crossing each other above the shimmering warmth of the summer Spanish sun in the hills whilst heading towards Galicia. How could two days be so different? The morning walk went well and at a brisk pace as we chatted about casual and friendly issues relating to the Camino and our reasons for undertaking the walk. We soon found ourselves entering the old town of Ponferada where on arrival we sat in the unusually clean and modern cafe by Spanish standards opposite the imposing castle once used and built by the Knights Templar. One conversation that surprised me was the subject of the Covid vaccine where both Eva from Prague and Olivier from Provence were vehemently opposed and dubious about the merits of the injection concentrating on the possible harms! How interesting that these Bohemian youngsters are so anti to the solution that was backed by virtually all national governments and peoples to solve the problem and keep the old living for longer than arguably was or is their natural time! I thought I was alone in thinking that when nature sends an occasional cull through a plague we shouldn't necessarily fight against it, especially when causing such harm to the young with their education and social skills which are so necessary for their development into adulthood. That said, I'm not completely against the vaccine and its merits. I've simply got an open mind to the arguments on either side and prepared to listen to the debate and opinions unlike my fellow walkers today.

From Ponferada we walked on and because of the fine weather soon found ourselves in the interesting town of Villafranca, a thirty kilometre day. My mood was good probably because of yesterday's bad weather experience and so nothing could dampen my spirits or so I thought! The municipal Albergue on the right hand side as we entered the town was sadly closed, it was suggested that some Albergues are still closed as a legacy to the Covid closures. We therefore checked into the next available accommodation on the opposite side of the road which was the lowest point of the Camino accommodation and truly dreadful. Looking back now as I relate the conditions I can smile and almost state that it was character building even for a man in his mid fifties and with a personality already fully formed! However this was a shock to the system and something I thought I would never experience. Having paid my seventeen euros which included the evening meal I was shown to the sleeping area which was a rusty bunk bed allocated to me on uneven flooring by an extremely overweight man. Nearby was a Frenchman with rags of filthy clothing strewn over the floor against his bed area. Oh well, it's only for one night I told myself heading for the shower. The freezing water trickled down as I thumped the pusher repeatedly and with shampoo suds still on me I was forced to abandon the wash. I entered the toilet for a much needed "number two" visit where to my horror after the deed was done there was no toilet paper of any kind. An angry shout from my concrete cell of a cracked seat above a hole brought no assistance and so the small covering of my micro towel was the only option before returning to the trickling water of the shower to attempt further cleaning of my rear end passage. My English reserve brought no verbal complaint, why would it? This is the Camino I told myself despite inwardly wondering how I would survive the night!

Assembling for dinner I was opposite Martha and I could tell she was as disgruntled and annoyed by the conditions as I but to our mutual surprise none of the the youngsters around us seemed to be disappointed or phased. I don't believe the young Camino pilgrims are more stoic or easily pleased and therefore I can only conclude they are oblivious to their surroundings. I suspected along with Martha that the dinner wouldn't be good and perhaps this would be the catalyst for the young and old to revolt in unison! The boiling brown water came to the table to be ladled out into the dirty soup bowls and looking down into the slop before me I could see small red pieces of Chorizo sausage against the bubbling water and through the film of grease on the surface. However, what brought a grimace of disgust to the face of my Swiss ally opposite me was the floating inch long pieces of gristly white fat bobbing about which brought our spoons from either side of the table to be laid down upon the long wooden bench before us. The younger pilgrims didn't seem phased or revolted by the sight although to be fair to Olivier and Julia abstaining through their vegetarian lifestyle why would they be?

The potato stodgy main course described as traditional Spanish Tortilla followed and then a small bowl of tinned fruit was eaten with a degree of relief that the soup terrines had left the table albeit with the aforementioned dirty bowls remaining to be used for the potato second course! For the first time on this Camino I was acutely aware of the difference between the generations in accepting these conditions, if it were not for Martha's presence and her clear display of annoyance I would seriously question my reason, judgement and cause for concern but the look on her face of disgust spoke volumes!

VILLAFRANCA TO LA FABA

29965 Steps

Chicken and Chips

The appalling and seemingly deliberate grunting and exhaling of air by the Frenchman sleeping nearby prevented a good night's sleep but fortunately this didn't ruin the day's walk that saw the sun shine brightly under a cloudless sky. I walked the first ten kilometres with Martha from Zurich Switzerland and we discussed openly the disgusting previous night's hostel before moving on to the beauty of her country where I am lucky enough to have visited often. However the main topic of conversation returned to the dreadful nights sleep that she too had suffered in the ladies dormitory, neither of us could understand the need for forced separation of the sexes unless to prevent an uprising that could have resulted in a monetary refund or the overweight scoundrels that ran the Albergue being lynched. Of course, I'm joking. No pilgrim would contemplate such behaviour and interestingly at the end of my Camino in Santiago de Compostela I sat drinking Vermouth cocktails with Martha and we almost found the experience at Villafranca on reflection amusing.

Our well earned coffee break came in a clean café along the Way where I took advantage of the services that had been lacking the night before and when leaving the Albergue that morning. When I returned from the café bathroom after a very successful visit Martha had been joined by two German sisters, Jacqueline from Berlin and Yvonne from Brunswick and soon followed by Fabian who was also from Berlin. I proudly used my pigeon-spoken German to great amusement and the two sisters and Fabian would feature greatly on my Camino walk, I could tell they would be great fun and entertaining company. As I introduced myself as Richard, Jacqueline immediately corrected my title to 'King' Richard. I can only assume she meant Richard the Lionheart of Robin Hood fame and not the other two who died in unpleasant circumstances with the latter being a hunchback and supposedly a child murderer! I knew instinctively that the Camino nickname would stick and that from now on I would be known as 'King Richard'. Sure enough later encounters with as yet unknown pilgrims would immediately on introduction say 'Oh, yes King Richard, I've heard of you.' I guess on the Camino it's a compliment to be known hopefully in this affectionate tone long before any encounter!

I walked on seeing a Camino sign stating that there was now just one hundred and sixty kilometres until Santiago de Compostela and I knew where I would spend the night before me prior to reaching the province of Galicia. I hoped to stay in the same Albergue that is run by German hospitaleros and that I remembered with affection on my previous visit nine years before although not necessarily run by the same hospitaleros. I therefore arrived alone at La Faba, a slightly shorter day, where the happy memories came flooding back as I recounted being here with Birgit and three Australian chums Richard, Pete and Warren. The Santa Marina La Faba is still run by the kindness of German hospitaleros, Roland and his wife Llona but with a mix of incredible Germanic efficiency, an amazing contrast to the absolute dregs I'd just experienced and that I won't mention again!

I'm joined by a lady, a French speaking lady cyclist, she surprisingly speaks no English which makes my efforts at Franglai look impressive.
"Bonjour Madame, Je suis Richard, Je suis Anglais!"
"Err" was the reply!
OK, best leave it there especially as I'm beginning to like some of the French folk that I've met thus far like Olivier and Pierre Henri and my experiences when travelling earlier through Paris

and then to Bayonne are now almost forgotten. There's a large Spanish pilgrim loitering around travelling by Mule and he seems to stop regularly for the local bars leaving his Mule to graze on the grass. As I look out on the lawn area I can see the Mule is currently near my drying washing hanging from the line so I guess there's a chance he may be sleeping here for the night, hopefully the large dormitory will help if he's snoring later and under the influence of the wine from the bar. Returning from the local hostelry having enjoyed, yet again, Chicken and Chips with Vino Tinto I'm pleased to see that man and beast have gone although this is unfair to the Mule who has done me no harm but I suspected that from the look of the rider I might be facing two consecutive nights of sleep deprivation with a noisy pilgrim snoring nearby.

Roland and Llona were sitting on a bench basking in the remains of the setting sun and I joined them discussing the mediaeval church opposite and the 'bell wall' as opposed to bell towers that are seen more widely on churches in other European countries. The French speaking cyclist arrived and interestingly I found I was not alone in finding her completely incomprehensible. The two host Germans and I were completely at a loss to fathom anything she said. However after what appeared a lengthy attempt we managed to ascertain that she was from Brugge Belgium and not France that I mistakenly and perhaps rudely assumed. We thought she was proud to state that the King of her country was currently walking the pilgrimage trail like us, perhaps I'll meet up with his Royal Highness of Belgium later where I'm sure he'll make more sense than his lively and jolly subject who by now is in full voice either discussing her bicycle route on the following day or a chocolate recipe from back home!

LA FABA TO TRIACASTELA

36314 Steps

Hamburger and Chips Vino Tinto

A truly wonderful day with fine weather and beautiful views uninterrupted for miles with perfect walking conditions. I left the La Faba hostel warmly sent on my way by the kindness of Llona and Roland. I received an encouraging email from Tongi who was by now nearing Santiago de Compostela, she had also spent the night at this hostel ahead of me by three or four days and the friendly Germans having seen her photograph shown by me on my iPhone were particularly pleased to see her still underway and asked me to pass on their best wishes should I meet Tongi again in the Galician city.

After an hour's walk I met Joseph originally from India but now living in Philadelphia as a Protestant preacher and he bore witness to his profession with a confident yet quiet and kind tone in his voice. We spoke at length and he was openly critical of the divisive US system of politics that acts vehemently against the other with equal venom whether Democrat or Republican. I was genuinely amazed as I was led to believe that the educated liberal elite worldwide despised Donald Trump and the Republicans through no other reason than their opposition to his very being regarding him as evil and it seems at times to be the Antichrist. Perhaps Joseph being an immigrant to the US had a better understanding of issues than those living in the States and brought up with the extremes of left and right. He also believed that this partisan system is dangerous for sound judgement on decisions relating to Ukraine or China's influence on the world stage whether good or bad. I was proud to say that I try to keep an open mind on these issues despite the unhealthy and biased influence of the media but I added my amusement towards Donald Trump who I likened to a comical cartoon character. Finally and at length we discussed the spiritual qualities of the Camino, the pull that encourages a few believers, many agnostics and even the confused atheists to put best foot forward often in discomfort for a longing need of fulfilment.

After leaving Joseph I met the Australian group again from two days prior in Molinaseca. Nick walked with me and we chatted about cricket, life in Brisbane and the damage to the barrier reef from global warming, the Chinese money now responsible and supporting much of Australian tourism and the life of the indigenous Aborigines now receiving reparations from the government to spend as they wish apparently not always well! At Triacastela I met Nor, a Dutch girl living in Spain who was sitting in the sun enjoying a cold drink whilst deciding which Albergue to choose. I had a lengthy chat with her about the book she was reading, Animal Farm by George Orwell that I recall from school lessons, sadly too many years ago than I care to remember, and its intended symbolism to the Bolshevik Menshevik struggles of the Russian revolution. An interesting girl that I hope to meet again on later travels which is quite likely with just seven stages left to travel.

At my chosen hostel were Lee, a South Korean, Sonno, another South Korean, Natsuki, a Japanese young girl and Sebastian from Paris. The latter had met Martin, the English pilgrim, many days before as had I so we instantly formed a friendly connection. Just prior to retiring for the night and retrieving my dried washing from the line I looked out at the evening setting sun on the Albergue balcony and was instantly overwhelmed by my amazing good fortune despite missing my wife Kathy. I feel extremely fit in body and mind and am truly blessed in this moment of contented contemplation and pleasure that I attribute to the location and the Camino but mostly to the people I have met today.

TRIACASTELA TO SARRIA

23984 Steps

Another fantastic day leaving the clean and delightful Albergue Limos in the beautiful setting of Triacastela in the Galician mountains. Once again the walking conditions were perfect and I enjoyed the first two hours in peace only passing one other pilgrim backpacker who I suspect was from a South American country by his accented response to the familiar greeting of Buen Camino. The views changed slightly with each period of descent and eventually I came across an Israeli girl that I'd met the previous day and Vicky from Washington DC. Vicky, I subsequently found, was a friend of the Australian Cheryl who I'd met earlier, apparently the two ladies were close friends from a previous Camino where they had first met in 2019. I wasn't surprised to learn that Cheryl had befriended this American lady or her two sisters also walking on this Camino that I met later, Cheryl had a personality that was infectious and instantly one would be attracted to. She was the amiable character that would easily find herself in the closest of friendships in quick time and one of those people desperately needed in wider society that facilitates friendly ties that are lasting. She is clearly the best of friends to all she meets, a wonderful presence in life and I wasn't surprised later to learn her vocation and calling was of a social worker.

Having left Vicky, with the promise of meeting her later in Sarria for a well earned drink I walked on meeting Lee and Natsuki who were resting on a grassy bank and then later Sonno who was walking alone. We walked together for an hour and exchanged mobile phone numbers as our conversation was centred around the growing number of pilgrims that we were now encountering at the sleeping hostels and Sonno showed some concern as to whether she'd find a bed each night. In truth she had more chances of success than I if there was an issue of accommodation with her ease of using APPS and modern technology but if she had a specific problem I'd do my best to assist. Having found accommodation in Sarria opposite the pilgrim office and after showering and washing clothes I wandered up the steep hill and into the old town where I found Cheryl calling out my name from a distance. We found a Cafe bar and spent an hour having a lengthy chat before being joined by Nick and Sue, Cheryl's Australian friends. Sonno had been successful in finding a bed but was alone when she walked past and therefore joined us in the warm summer's night which provided the perfect atmosphere of Camino spirit and restfulness.

This night would lead to one of the most enjoyable evenings of my entire month's experience whilst walking the Camino. On the inspiration and due to the infectious nature of Cheryl one by one a succession of pilgrims arrived to swell our ever growing number so within a further hour we were joined by John from England, Jaana from Finland, Gordon from Ireland but living in Durham England and Mike from Canada but living in Japan. By this point any lone pilgrim, some newly arrived to walk the final hundred kilometres, in need of friendly encouragement for their pilgrim walk the following day or tempted by a glass of wine and accompanied by some Galician cheese on the table was forming a crowd outside the bar and on the cobbles. All of the assembled party became familiar faces that I would encounter over the next few days of walking. I reflected in amazement how many different nationalities and people from all demographics can meet outside a Spanish bar and street soaking up the magic that is the Camino spirit. It wasn't the wonderful Galician cheese or the flowing icy Alborino wine that brought us together or indeed solely the magic of the Camino, it was Cheryl who oozed through every fibre of her being what it means to be a Camino pilgrim, welcoming and kind to all around. Full of good cheer, Bon Ami and memories of lasting humour I returned to my bed knowing that I may sleep deeply with heavy dreams fuelled by the excess of cheese and wine!

SARRIA TO PORTOMARIN

33396 Steps

Peanuts and fruit

What an incredible day and another one that will live with me for a long while. Leaving my Sarria accommodation I walked for a few hundred yards before recognising Eliia from Moscow ahead of me. I passed with a greeting but she stopped me and mentioned the German sisters she had encountered the night before in the Sarria municipal Albergue who were talking affectionately, I assume, about "King Richard" from England. Of course I knew Jacqueline, Yvonne and Fabian from Germany and so unless there is another "King Richard" walking the Camino it could only be me they were discussing. The topic was humorous enough for Eliia and I to smile and then walk together for the whole day. Eliia was very good company and lived a full and fascinating life in Moscow along with spending a great deal of time visiting an area near my home in Kent England through her work and so we instantly formed a connection. How similar I thought we are in nature with an interest in music ranging from the classical of Rachmaninov, Tchikovski and Glazinov to the rock band Queen. I was surprised to learn that Eliia runs the Russian fan club for Queen and has met the now knighted guitarist Brian May personally. I mentioned my watching a live Queen concert at the old Wembley Stadium London after the famous Live Aid performance in the 1980s many years ago with Freddie Mercury singing energetically and our Camino friendship was strengthened further. This in itself isn't unusual other than the fact of the Ukraine war dividing the Western propaganda from that of the Russian and it reminded me how in a globalised age how similar we are in culture and how ridiculous I feel the war is to have escalated to this extent from a regional spat of nationalism to one that is now on the world stage. Eliia spoke of her childhood holidays in Crimea and trips to Kiev as a youngster to sing Ukrainian folk songs in the capital's cathedral.

As we walked further the time passed quickly and my admiration for Eliia grew, she is without doubt one of the most exceptional ladies I've ever met and certainly on this Camino. She has an appreciation of the arts, composes music and plays the piano, she is currently building her own house, has self funded her education to reach the top of her pharmaceutical profession and is a qualified Psychologist with a degree. By the end of the day she had helped me with Albergue accommodation searches due to my lack of technical mobile phone APP skills that I mention sadly too often here. I seriously doubt that there is anything beyond her talents. She is widely travelled and told me of her experiences climbing Mount Sinai during the cold night and then watching the sunrise along with her hobby of diving in the waters around Egypt. I'd like to walk more with Eliia as I'm clearly impressed by her amazing talents and qualities but there is an intriguing distance between us as she retains an air of mystery. She mentioned that on the anticipated day of arrival in Santiago de Compostela she would reach a landmark birthday and I suggested a group celebration along with other pilgrims now known mutually to us but she coolly said that in Russia the particular birth year wasn't celebrated traditionally. It sounded like an excuse, I obviously accepted her Camino privacy but later found out that it was indeed bad luck to celebrate the occasion in Russian culture. I'll never forget the experience of today and the conversations we shared not least because as I suspected there are two sides to every story and the endless dripping of propaganda that I'm subjected to I believe doesn't tell the whole story of the Ukraine conflict. I'm no supporter of awful Russian aggression but if evidence were needed of the one sided argument then a simple question can be asked in my home country, why has the TV channel "Russia Today " been taken off air?

View of the River Mino at Portomarin

PORTOMARIN TO PALAIS DEL REI

34686 Steps

Chicken in mushroom sauce with potatoes and Santiago cake

A terrific day walking in yet more perfect conditions, cool to begin with but soon in the sunshine and warmth. The scenery has changed from mountains to hills over the last few days and now is the rolling, more gentle slopes and attractive countryside more familiar to the green fields of the South Downs found in England. It's interesting to see the resurgence of the occasional bright yellow rape seed field occasionally disrupting the beautiful landscape and when in close proximity giving off the foul sickly odour. It was often explained to me that the European Union subsidies to farmers encouraged the planting of this bilious sight for animal feed along with the pleasant cooking oil. Rather like wind turbines the yellow fields may offend the vista to many onlookers but if it's beneficial to mankind then I can live happily with it and the propeller blades although preferably from a distance!

The previous evening I'd not been able to join the group for dinner as planned and intended. My Albergue host had directed me to a top bunk bed that was an obstacle course to reach and I knew I would be required to climb over several French ladies rucksacks strewn around the floor near their beds. Added to this, I was sleeping above a South Korean girl who had placed drying clothes as an extra trip hazard with her belongings hanging from the rungs of my ladder up to the least accessible bed in the dormitory of twenty five beds. I therefore decided that dining out and a late return would be an impossible task in the certain darkness that would be imposed by the most tired or miserable of pilgrims in need of sleep. My lateness would have surely led to angry pilgrims and so I made the decision to abandon the evening meal and consequently whilst I walked in the morning Spanish sun my stomach was rumbling angrily.

After an hour's walk I saw Janet, a Canadian lady who was a guest at last night's dinner table and so I apologised for my absence. She appeared keen to chat and we spent the day walking together with my occasional input but mostly my listening to her personal life and home circumstances in Canada. She faced a dilemma concerning her working employment status in a medical setting considering whether to leave as she'd been moved to an internal office which lacked a window; it had been suggested that her many house plants scattered around shouldn't be allowed in a clinical environment. More personal issues followed from her lips and I thought this to be a compliment, with my experience as a seasoned Camino pilgrim I was happy that I may be a shoulder to cry on figuratively speaking. As with all the personal conversations made I wouldn't divulge them here or indeed anywhere else, no one would be interested anyway and it's obvious that we all have complicated lives! It was however strange to hear Janet telling another pilgrim on the following day the same lengthy story which left me wondering whether my listening had helped her domestic home life healing process.

After the walk that appeared more tiring than I had anticipated I arrived at the Albergue with Janet still at my side. Eliia had booked my accommodation on the previous day and was hopefully still on route but I was heartened and relieved to see the friendly group of Germans and Joseph from Philadelphia. We all enjoyed a good pilgrim dinner at a nearby restaurant where photographs were taken by the amiable hosts joined by the chef after a further bottle of wine had arrived making another memorable evening. Fabian from Berlin, who has an events management company, offered to book my accommodation for the following night as my hotel booking APP was still failing. It's easy to develop an inferiority complex believing that modern technology and the digital age has not been kind to me but I genuinely ask myself why if something can go wrong with an electronic gadget then it will for me! Thankfully the kindness of pilgrims like Fabian and Eliia came to my aid and whilst being overwhelmed I've learnt to not question the Camino generosity but simply to accept it as most pilgrims do with the shared sentiment being that "the Camino provides". And yet obviously I have a heartfelt appreciation towards these kind souls although Joseph made reference that my own nature played a part!

The following day is a planned twenty nine kilometre walk with dry conditions until some rain in the evening and therefore in the knowledge of a good day to come with accommodation booked and now with a contented stomach I entered my sleeping pod in the modern converted dormitory along with my fellow cosmopolitan pilgrims. My body has become accustomed to the long walks each day and with the added enjoyment of the now familiar company for the first time the thought of arriving at Santiago de Compostela, whilst still being a relief and a sense of accomplishment, may also be tinged with sadness at the Camino's ending.

PALAIS DEL REI TO AZURA

37726 Steps

The forecast was correct with good walking conditions for the first three quarters of the day before the annoying heavy rain would come. I walked alone, as was my custom, knowing that I would meet later with Camino friends in the various hostelries strategically placed along the Camino route amongst the growing numbers of pilgrims who had started from the shorter distance of the walk that starts in Sarria. The atmosphere and feeling in each hostelry is now markedly different as Sebastian from Paris discussed with me when we met at the first Cafe bar on route. I saw him in the first crowded seating area of the day's walk, the only familiar pilgrim face and I could see he had the same sense of bewilderment towards the new pilgrim faces around him. I'd initially met Sebastian when entering Galicia and he seemed somewhat downhearted at the change from seasoned and weary pilgrims who had walked literally hundreds of miles to the new trekkers who appeared to be on guided holiday tours! The newcomers obviously have the same right as all others but their excitable laughter and bubbling energy before the difficulties of the Camino with blisters and aching limbs can be slightly gawling. When one passes an elderly person who is cautiously walking gingerly over the sometimes rocky paths in sandals and without a rucksack one has mixed emotions of whether to feel admiration for their brave labours or wonder why they are putting themselves through the still arduous shorter part of the journey.

I passed an Irish lady named Jean who was clearly showing signs of distress and said that blisters were already forming despite it being just her third very short day of walking. I wasn't surprised as I glanced at the shape of her exposed, sock covered, toes through what appeared to be flip flops albeit with a strap around the heel area! Having experienced the same blister problem albeit after many miles I was sympathetic and offered her my now spare Compeed blister plasters that form a skin layer over the wound. In her strong Irish accent I could tell that she wanted to be stoic and brave and decline but I reassured her of the plaster's merits and with my Burgos experience and tale conveyed she soon accepted gratefully. I hope with my small degree of help that she completed the hundred kilometres remaining and if successful she would certainly deserve her credential. Who am I, or any other pilgrim, to judge the reasons or efforts required to complete the pilgrimage regardless of distance or indeed whether they achieve it laden down with a weighty rucksack or not or indeed inappropriate footwear!

I walked on passing through farm villages and some run down areas of the countryside where many properties were showing "for sale" signs, I was later informed that this was a legacy from the Covid 19 pandemic where the Camino pilgrimage routes were abandoned with the closure of many accommodation hostels. And yet there are more pilgrims now than my previous walk nearly ten years prior so if the poverty and decline is related to the pandemic it can only be that the local people and businesses couldn't recover in time. I suspect there's now an opportunity for newcomers and fresh businesses to arrive and rejuvenate the area as the Camino appeal shows no sign of stopping.

I passed, once again as I had previously, Vickey from America with a brief chat about her profession as a lawyer before her retirement and that her husband prefers to play tennis rather than walk. She was therefore here with her sisters who like me are encouraged to walk ahead for fear we would be slowed down by accompanying her. She is an inspiration to all other potential pilgrims who may believe themselves incapable of the Camino routes as her walking is indeed slow and with obvious difficulties due to an unknown cause and so must require extra determination and effort. Vickey has walked at least two previous Camino's from start to finish and is an example to us all that whatever speed is chosen and for whatever reason the pace of the pilgrimage can be done by those brave enough to simply begin.

As I walked on I came across two familiar ladies from the previous day Karen and Denise also from America, Texas and Pennsylvania respectively. Both ladies were very interesting to walk with, having different attitudes than one would expect from yet another professional lawyer, in this case Karen. It was a pleasure to chat with them and their appearance suggested they were new pilgrims starting from Sarria but no, they had endured and walked from the start like myself in St Jean Pied de Port and were by now seasoned pilgrims with similar stories to tell of their experiences. The mistake I made was wrongly judging their appearance from their facial cosmetics and youthful looks thinking them to be newly setting out contrasted against my tired, dishevelled and partially bearded state. The familiarity of the Camino allowed me to comment on their appearance being reminiscent of the start of a night out in the glitz of a fine restaurant or a nightclub albeit in walking clothes and with rucksacks. They laughed, was I flirting with them as is a weakness of mine or simply telling the truth! Either way we walked together for the rest of the day and had amusing conversations mixed with a current United States topical issue that the politically correct like to call "reproductive choice" and others call abortion. Karen supported the argument whereas Denise believed it should be made illegal. How interesting once again that these pilgrims had strong views and convictions on either side of the argument unlike myself who simply said in polite response to the conversation that "abortion shouldn't be relied upon as a last resort contraceptive". As with many discussions whilst walking this Camino I can see a complicated grey area where others show no signs of considering the other point of view and I'm beginning to wonder whether my open mindedness is possibly a failing of mine. If I had more acceptance without question for common ideas forced upon us by those in power or the way modern culture pushes the social norms would I be a more contented person? Would I be more tolerant of what's stated by those in authority or indeed those rebelling however strange and bizarre it appears at times on either side of the issues.

The time I spent with Karen and Denise passed quickly, they were good fun. But the anticipated rain was looming as the sky turned from a light grey to a darker shade of purple in the distance that we were walking towards. Sure enough the procession of pilgrims around me were becoming soaked and any further discussion with my American friends came to an abrupt end. We cowered in a corrugated plastic shelter until heading off until reaching our destination five miles away where I said my goodbyes to fellow travellers who were destined for other hostels. After a hot shower and rolling out my sleeping bag on yet another top bunk bed I met Roberta from Uruguay who was in a bunk bed nearby and to my surprise said he lived in Bromley Kent and commuted to London each day for work. How strange to find a fellow pilgrim that I had recognised and acknowledged over the last two hundred miles to now find he was domiciled in my home county!

The evening meal was the usual fun, how could it not be with Jacqueline from Berlin whose presence in any environment adds greatly to the occasion. Tonight our group is joined by Lena, a Swedish lady who has a mischievous laugh and especially after my lame attempts at cracking jokes. She says that the Swedish love the English sense of humour which to my childish nature is a green light to continue! Three bottles of red wine amongst the six of us was sufficient to add greatly to the pilgrim experience but like all good walkers knowing that the following day would be another thirty kilometre stroll with some steep slopes to negotiate along the way the evening enjoyment came to an orderly end.

AZURA TO LAVACOLLA

38734 Steps

German style home cooked food

Another amazing, terrific day. I set off this morning after breakfast with Janet from Canada and Lena from Sweden walking through the outskirts of Azura where we met Joseph from Philadelphia who appeared to be in a mischievous mood as he related a story of how he played devil's advocate with a Protestant group the day before. Joseph didn't divulge his deep rooted Christian faith but instead tried to get them to simply say that a belief in Jesus as their saviour was indeed their belief and conviction. We live in strange times where people are happy to bear witness with good deeds but only up until a point where the final declaration of their devout belief in Christ presumably leads to a premature ending of a conversation perhaps because modern culture and film drama portrays Christians routinely as very odd characters! I like Joseph very much, he has an incredible talent in his softly spoken tone to give a profound message of his own belief, faith and profession. I can imagine the game and dance he played with the Protestant group trying simply to allow them to discuss their faith without the perceived embarrassment and stigma involved in simply saying, we are Christians, open up your hearts and join us.

After Joseph's departure it was apparent that Janet wished to discuss some personal issues that she had mentioned to me prior, this time with Lena and so I discreetly raised my walking pace leaving them in peace and before long I found myself a good distance ahead despite sheltering from some heavy rain in the beautiful countryside and scenery that reminded me of

Cornwall back home in England. Janet was a kind and interesting character with strong views as she stated her admiration for the US president Joe Biden saying he is "a very clever and intelligent man"! My initial reaction wanted to laugh openly thinking she must surely be playing a joke on me but apparently not! The polling and media reports that come out of the United States suggest that the next election will be a choice of the "better of two evils", truly awful candidates, indeed even the most ardent of democrat supporters apparently wouldn't wholly endorse Joe Biden because of his many gaffes and obvious signs of forgetfulness in old age. But who am I to question Janet's strong belief in the qualities of the leader of "the free world" in this parallel universe that I am walking through and is the magic of the Camino de Santiago!

Jacqueline, Yvonne and Fabian were at the hostel on my arrival and a very friendly and some would say earthy natured Italian gentleman pilgrim from Venice named Roger. Roger was in the adjacent bunk bed allocated to me and after the usual ritual of rolling out the sleeping bag and showering I asked Roger if he was also in need of a Vino Tinto and we were soon departing for a nearby bar that to my surprise Roger had used before on his many previous pilgrimages. Over two very enjoyable glasses of Rioja Roger told me of his wild and youthful adventures in South America selling wines from Europe and how he'd first entered into the Sommelier business by working initially as a young waiter at the Dorchester hotel in London before moving on to the wine sales business. However Covid had not been kind to Roger and so he was back home in Europe walking the Camino yet again seemingly through boredom before finding new employment. His stories of relationship encounters with women over the years were entertaining and whilst risqué perhaps to some more naive and innocent ears they were delivered with such humour that I found myself grinning widely probably because I realised that there was perhaps something of an exaggeration and embellishment about the accuracy!

Having enjoyed a third Vino Tinto, my mobile phone rang. Jacqueline was vocally but kindly telling me, with a perhaps surprising summons, to return to the communal dining table at the hostel where a huge spread of home cooked delights had been prepared and laid out. I took a chance and invited the as yet uninvited Roger back for dinner to the pilgrim gathering and of course he was welcomed with open arms by the German sisters, Lena and Janet who had also played a huge part in the spread of food. This was another example of the amazing Pilgrim Camino spirit of hospitality as without question Roger on arrival was invited to the table and as the food was enjoyed by the already large group two young ladies from the Czech Republic joined us squeezing into the gaps being made.

My summons to the dining table by Jacqueline I accepted as one that would be made by a sisterly or motherly kindness despite us being of similar age. I really can't say why so many people mother me with such kindness unless I convey a sense or impression of helplessness which is entirely possible and even perhaps somewhat true! Do I look like a little boy lost? Is it possible that I like being helped so much and accepting assistance without question? I think, and I'm actually not ashamed to say, that I do, I like female company around me and if they see me as a little boy lost and a worthy cause then so be it.

The evening meal had a terrific and typical Camino atmosphere. I sat in the middle of the table with Yvonne to my left and Janet to my right, Lena opposite and with Jacqueline to her side and our new friend Roger at the head of the table was clearly grateful to be introduced to this intimate but swelling gathering. Fabian, who was nearest to the kitchen area, willingly played the part of waiter as the dinner plates were removed and the dessert courses arrived before coffee and chocolates pleasantly rounded off the evening's fair. Ooni from Tokyo Japan and currently on her European leg of a long vacation joined us sitting with the Czech girls and we all planned tomorrow's shorter walk of just 10 kilometres. We would arrive in Santiago de Compostela together, early enough to appreciate almost a full day collecting our Compostela certificates, witnessing the Pilgrim Mass in the Cathedral and enjoying the delights of the wonderful city.

LAVACOLLA TO SANTIAGO DE COMPOSTELA

28969 Steps

Fish Stew Platter

It was an easy ten kilometre walk that was required to reach the centre of Santiago de Compostela and despite the poor weather forecast the conditions remained ideal being cool and dry albeit overcast for the walk that was an exciting climax to the whole venture. Only the bizarre decision making of individual pilgrims could change the plan that we could all arrive together that was agreed and discussed the night before. We had arranged to enter the cobblestone area where newly arriving pilgrims traditionally gather to take photographs, pat each other on the back, embrace and wallow in the magnificent achievement that is the endurance test and realisation of what we had just accomplished. Sure enough, plans already made deviated and trips to Albergues for prearranged accommodation on route altered the arrangements. Fabian arrived at the square ahead of the group with a faster pace where he met Roger from Italy who had also marched ahead with his long striding legs.

A decision to store bags at the monastery hostel on route delayed the larger group further but eventually we arrived at this special and magical place where the earlier pilgrim friends were waiting with anticipated excitement for us. This probably resulted in a more heightened and pleasurable experience as we were cheered loudly and greeted with smiles and embraces by Fabian and Roger. I walked in with the enchanting Yvonne (Wonny) from Germany who I'd become close to during the previous few days, the archetypal stern German character wrongly believed by the

British couldn't be further from the truth with regard to Wonny who's humour and relaxed nature had greatly added to my Camino experience. Jaqueline followed closely behind with Lena from Sweden and cheers, handshakes and hugs soon followed before the customary group photographs with the twin Cathedral towers proudly rising behind us for the imposing backdrop. Familiar pilgrim faces entered the square and were mixed with those already known to us that were soaking in the atmosphere of pure joy, relief and satisfaction. All around me were scattered groups of pilgrims from different nationalities airing their delight with the occasional lone pilgrim breaking off after their celebrations and pictures to sit in reflection of their own personal reasons for the pilgrimage, perhaps in memory of others possibly recently bereaved or separated from them.

Roger from Italy turned out to be of far more significance and impact than I could ever have imagined. As I mentioned above he had walked the many Camino routes to Santiago de Compostela, he proudly said that this was his fifteenth Camino and with his wide knowledge he began to recommend the procedure of how we should get our Compostela certificates, where to sit in the Cathedral for the best viewing experience and appreciate the swinging of the Botafumeiro that traverses through the naive of the Cathedral belching incense into the air for the astounded congregation. We successfully received our Compostelas without queuing as Roger suggested and then attended the pilgrim mass which, despite being my second time of witnessing, is a very moving and inspiring experience. I was left with the strong sense and thought as I looked on observing the mass and spectacle that this Christian celebration matters and has a profound meaning that can only be the certain hope of the existence of God.

Roger, who I was beginning to see comically and affectionately as a benevolent tour guide, knew the best wine bars serving the finest vino, the best Galician fish restaurants and was on hand to answer any number of questions that either individually or collectively were asked concerning Camino life or that of the city. He imparted this kindness in a manner that wasn't intrusive and I think all considered his insightful knowledge as being genuinely good and very much appreciated. We visited the restaurant where he knew the staff, ordered wine and food, and I shared the Fish Stew dish with Jaqueline whilst the others picked at the shell fish delicacies placed at the centre of the table. Extra local Alberino wine arrived which was well received and especially in the moment by me, however in hindsight this was my one and only slight reservation towards Rogers's amiable persuasive nature. For my part and from a weakness of character I have to admit that I could have done without the extra bottles of fine wine brought to the table. Roger, being an expert in this vintner field, had encouraged me to overindulge at the restaurant and again once some of the other pilgrims had wisely decided to return to their beds after the meal. The German sisters accompanied Roger and myself to yet another bar where a very fine bottle of Rioja was enjoyed which arrived with a complimentary platter of Galician cheese and Salami meats. Wonny and Jacqueline finally and sensibly departed but Roger knew that I would love to try a particular Rioja of his recommendation and of course I did! The ensuing headache that followed the following morning was obviously my own fault.

The discomfort I felt when waking from my hotel bed was soon gone as I recalled the pleasant evening from the night before, the conversations I'd had with Roger when we were last to leave the bar, I suspect, much to the relief of the staff! It was my previous invitation, the day before, to Roger for him to join me in a glass of Vino Tinto and this introduction he said had made his Camino experience so enjoyable, especially meeting the exceptionally larger than life character that is Jacqueline. Roger hugged me closely as we departed with a wine induced over affectionate embrace on the cobbles of the square next to the floodlit Cathedral and he thanked me deeply and emotionally. In this moment, perhaps fuelled by the wine and the Camino spirit, I felt genuinely pleased that I'd been a pivotal part in his final part of this Camino Way with the mere simple act of an overture and invitation for a drink. I've since been in email contact with Roger who's search in Italy for employment is continuing and therefore with spare time I suspect he's on or planning another Camino as I write.

After a morning of recovery and relaxation I met Wonny and Fabian in the Cathedral square and we bought the tickets for the guided tour that visited the rooftop of the St James Basilica to appreciate the views of the city from above. The reddish brown tiles shone in the midday sun and we each enjoyed the elevated position whilst taking photographs and hearing the guide tell the story of the Apostle St James and the many Camino routes that culminated directly beneath where we stood on the concrete slabbed roofing. We three grinning pilgrims with the stunning background of Santiago de Compostela behind took several more pictures from all four sides of the Cathedral when a tourist from South America looked towards me and offered to take a group photograph of me flanked by my two German pilgrim friends. As the picture was taken Wonny and Fabian in unison made reference to standing beside "King Richard" on the roof that brought a wide smile to my face and a lasting Camino memory.

St James Basilica rooftop

Santiago de Compostela Cathedral - meeting place and end of the traditional route, although many pilgrims now walk on until they reach the Atlantic

MY REFLECTIONS

My personal thoughts and reflections of this Camino experience as I write three days after arriving in Santiago de Compostela and from my luxurious hotel room are interesting but strangely difficult to write as I am now alone. The pilgrims I had walked with have departed back to their home countries and despite the magical setting that is Santiago de Compostela and the daily atmosphere of delight very evident from newly arriving pilgrims, for me it is now tinged with a degree of loss. This is obviously inevitable and I must concentrate on the brighter future before me but I am not alone in these feelings as a pilgrim from Germany named Johannes is perhaps grieving more than I after making deeper friendships over a longer period. Johannes didn't walk with me, he and I have only just met but there is an empathy between us as he has made deep connections that have come to an abrupt end as they surely must. I consoled him by saying that I remain friends with the pilgrims that I had met nine years before which brought a small smile to his face.

I will break up my reflections into three parts, firstly the physical then the spiritual and finally the personal aspects and how my character may have changed from the experience as inevitably it has. It's not possible to walk away from home for this amount of time and distance without at the very least forming strong memories, even if it's nothing more than remembering the discomfort and pain which brings me neatly to the first category.

The physical and practical aspect of the Camino I would sum up as very different from my previous experience nearly ten years prior. The first obvious difference is the common and widely used mobile phone APPS relating to the Camino where details of hostels, Albergues, hotels and services are widely available and shared between pilgrims. The trusted John Brierly guidebook so well thumbed and evident on my previous Camino is now a rare sight replaced by readily available and immediately updated information in real time on devices in each pilgrims hand or Cargo trouser pockets. The Camino APPS link to Google maps so it's now virtually impossible to be lost regardless of the many Yellow arrow markers or Scallop shell signs pointing the Way. Perhaps the signage will eventually be lost and no longer needed as the travellers look to their mobile phones for directions and in doing so miss the landscape and views in the process! Will the guide books and Camino written accounts belong to a bygone era as Camino pilgrims now film their experiences on YouTube often accompanied by tears of pain or joy to encourage the viewers to show either sympathy or humour depending on their gullibility! The pilgrims that I met all had the technical ability, unlike me, to book their dormitory beds ahead leaving me to rely on newly made friends and fellow pilgrims for their understanding of "mobile apps". Whilst accepting the kindness of my Camino fellow walkers as they booked accommodation for me and themselves I can honestly say that regardless of their digital talents and their use of Camino APPS I liked their company and would have walked, talked and toiled with them willingly rather than be alone. I enjoyed an hour or two of solitude for the initial part of the day and before the first resting cafe but not for longer. It should be stated that I've always tried hard to understand and use modern digital technology but if something can go wrong then it will for me as was proven by my booking.com experience that failed after the second successful use. Apparently an issue between the bank card provider and APP!

If I had to say what is required physically to walk the Camino I would say hiking boots for the Pyrenees and Galician hills, I would say trekking lightweight shoes for the flat Maseta. I would say a warm sleeping bag for the early hours of the morning and a light sleeping bag for the warm period at turning in for the night. I would say a warm fleece and long trousers for the cold in the high altitude and early mornings from daybreak until nine o'clock. I would say shorts and T shirts for the hot midday sun and afternoons. In other words if you can get everything needed that I've mentioned above into your rucksack, amongst all other needed items such as toiletries, then you are a better person or certainly more skilled at packing than I am but this is the challenge of the Camino!

From a spiritual aspect this Camino as before is fascinating, there is in my opinion nothing spectacular about the landscape when compared to the Alps, the Norwegian Fjords, the Italian lakes or any other number of world renowned areas of natural beauty and tourist destinations from around the world. So what is it that brings pilgrims and walkers back often for multiple times to walk the way of St James? My belief is that there has to be a magnetic pull on the soul that the atheists don't acknowledge question or appreciate, that the agnostics accept as something spiritually undefined or unfathomable but believe the Camino is a truly magical force of nature and finally that those with a Christian faith understand the pull without question as they do with every aspect of their Christian belief and teachings.

As I walked the Way I felt the spirit of goodness in the pilgrim's I met and the incredible kindness of the hospitalaro's from England, Fiona and Ray, and from Germany Llona and Roland. I felt the presence of God in Leon Cathedral and at the Santiago de Compostela Mass which despite giving me a strong emotional sensation brought no increase or profound change or revelation to my outlook on life. Maybe it should have left a greater intensity but as I already believe that I am blessed and aware of the presence of God's grace, despite my many flaws and sins, my heightened emotions in the Cathedrals or witnessing of the kind acts of others around me I accept as nothing more than the further confirmation of God's love and presence. However, I know I should bear witness and change my selfish ways! On this Camino walk when compared with the last time I met far fewer pilgrims walking for Christian or religious reasons, only the Spanish girl Paula and Joseph from Philadelphia when asked or in conversation believed and spoke openly of their faith.

Has the Camino changed me? It is probably only a question that others can answer from their observations but in some ways I can say that it has. I've lost well over a stone in weight, possibly explained by my gluten intolerance forbidding pasta and an excess of bread and pastries which was ever present in the communal kitchens and Albergues. Or could my weight loss be explained by the very bad and on occasion truly awful meals I encountered forcing me to abstain completely on some days and rely on fruit and nuts but always accompanied by the ever present Vino Tinto! I'm sure health professionals wouldn't advise walking such long distances without a healthy diet and certainly wouldn't recommend the amount of sociable drinking of alcohol but the end result is I now feel fitter and healthier in body with my reduced weight and for this reason alone the experience has been thoroughly worthwhile.

I am enormously encouraged by the youngsters I met who without exception are the finest of well meaning and kind individuals that one would ever wish to meet. It has truly been a privilege to encounter each one who is either entering or already a member of a useful profession in employment that can be offered up to the glory of God or humanity. I will always remember conversations with Bethany from Washington DC entering into the psychiatry profession, Aparna from Boston training as a virologist, Daniel also from Boston who having returned from volunteering in a refugee camp in Poland was bound for useful employment in agriculture, Michel from Denmark and Johannes from Germany currently working with young adults with learning difficulties such as Asperger's and Down syndrome. Another fine example was Julia from Amsterdam with a seemingly endless passionate outlook and optimism of how she can introduce ethical policies into the banking system. Olivier and

Eva both had an enthusiasm for their more bohemian lifestyles that was centred on social kindness and were welcoming of my presence. All of the above never made me feel my age amongst them, they made me as welcome as any other member of the Camino community despite my traditional views or slower speed in comprehending the youthful culture that they embraced.

The more senior pilgrims I encountered were possibly more complex which probably isn't surprising as with age comes cynicism, heartache, loss and depression where some more personal stories were relayed over the long days and evenings in discussions which details aren't for this account. However the one recurring thought that occurs to me now when looking back and reflecting upon my experiences is one I find most fascinating and one that my friends at home will find hilarious if they were to read it here. I am far more "open minded" than virtually everyone, young and old, I encountered! For instance on issues such as climate change, the Covid pandemic and the current cultural topic of inclusion everyone I met had a definitive opinion.

On the issue of climate change and whether human impact can prevent it I honestly don't know and said so as opposed to all others. One lady stated it had become an "extreme religion for fanatics" before making her disparaging views known about the environmentalist and activist Greta Thurnberg. Many others certainly believed it was an issue of importance and spoke passionately in favour of taking drastic action but weren't prepared to change their behaviour which included further planned flights from across the world to walk the ancient path to Santiago de Compostela or any manner of other exotic destinations on the world tourist must see list. One gentleman became quite animated with his strongly held beliefs and views on humans changing their behaviour advocating mass use of wind turbines and ownership of electric vehicles but laughably had no intention of changing his lifestyle that proudly owned both a second home for holidays and a larger diesel vehicle to visit the said property which necessitated a long car journey.

On the subject of Covid yet again many spoke with certainty concerning its bizarre origin being either man made from a laboratory in China or mutating from bats to animals and subsequently to humans. Each opposing view then discussed in certainties the dangers to health from the vaccine followed by their refusal to take it or conversely others spoke of the stupidity of those not eager to be first in line. The opinions ranged between the necessities of discrimination inflicted against individuals who fiercely refused the vaccines use to the alternative view that those refusing should be dismissed from employment. Unlike the group of Camino pilgrims that I encountered I have no idea where Covid originated and I suspect like many politicians who took the vaccine willingly or perhaps reluctantly neither do they.

Amongst the more senior pilgrims and perhaps this is reflected elsewhere in wider society and not just on the Camino trail there is a reluctance to accept changes where current gender issues are not understood properly in the area of inclusivity. Some were clearly becoming frustrated by the speed of change where a new pronoun or letter is added to the list of categories before the last one has been explained and embedded into mainstream culture. Yet again I consider myself to have an "open mind" on this matter and perhaps align myself with some of the more disinterested youthful sect where I recall the laughter and expression from young Daniel from America as he threw his head back and said, "we don't really care!" My own view is people can call themselves what they want unless there is an insistence that the downright bizarre becomes the norm!

Finally have I become a better person, a more tolerant person, a kinder person? I can't say, maybe the test will be when I arrive home and when the usual annoying distractions of life will resume fuelled by the ever growing media excitement of the latest disaster to hit the news headlines. On one subject and one alone, and reflecting on my Pamplona experience when witnessing the awful cruelty to the horse, I can say sadly my level of intolerance towards this man has not changed. Despite many believing miracles happen on the Camino de Santiago my anger towards this individual and the Spanish culture at large of cruelty to animals remains, any country that takes delight in organised entertainment of Bullfighting and then televises it I believe is beyond belief! However, the experience of meeting some very special people will live with me forever and I hope these memories over time may mellow my nature. Thanks especially to Jacqueline, Wonny, Fabian, Cheryl, Tongi, Eliia, Donnacha, Carmel, Martha and Roger whose company made a particular and lasting impression.

Jack, Mikel, Christian... Denmark
Carmel, Nick, Sue, Cheryl, Greg, Keith... Australia
Barbara, Lena... Sweden
Satu, Tanya, Jose... Finland
Sophie, Nor, Muk, Julia... Netherlands
Tongi ... Austria
Jacqueline, Yvonne, Fabian, Torban, Nick, Johannes ... Germany
Eliia... Russia
Eva ... Czech Republic
Olivier, Valentine, Gale, Bastion... France
Joseph, Karen, Denise, Daniel, Lochlan, Vicky, Kathy, Terry, Aparna, Bethany... USA
Paula, Daniel... Spain
Mike, Jean Claud, Jo, Janet... Canada
Donnacha, Cormac Gordon, Anne, John... Ireland
Sono, Solo, Lee... South Korea
Ooni, Natsuki, Satu... Japan
Roberta... Uruguay
John, Martin... England
Marta, Gunter, Walter... Switzerland
Marie, Bob... Belgium
Becky... Wales
Maana, Lisa... Israel

Hospitalarios. English... Fiona, Ray, Anne
Hospitalarios German... Roland, Llona

Apologies to all those not mentioned above, you all made it a memorable, worthwhile and an enjoyable time for me.

Printed in Great Britain
by Amazon

47537253R10066